BRIGHT NOTES

THE ODYSSEY BY HOMER

Intelligent Education

Nashville, Tennessee

BRIGHT NOTES: The Odyssey
www.BrightNotes.com

No part of this publication may be used or reproduced in any manner whatsoever without written permission, except in the case of brief quotations in critical articles and reviews. For permissions, contact Influence Publishers http://www.influencepublishers.com.

ISBN: 978-1-645422-28-0 (Paperback)
ISBN: 978-1-645422-29-7 (eBook)

Published in accordance with the U.S. Copyright Office Orphan Works and Mass Digitization report of the register of copyrights, June 2015.

Originally published by Monarch Press.
David Sider; David Konstan; Robert Shorter, 1963
2020 Edition published by Influence Publishers.

Interior design by Lapiz Digital Services. Cover Design by Thinkpen Designs.

Printed in the United States of America.

Library of Congress Cataloging-in-Publication Data forthcoming.
Names: Intelligent Education
Title: BRIGHT NOTES: The Odyssey
Subject: STU004000 STUDY AIDS / Book Notes

CONTENTS

1)	Introduction to Homer	1
2)	Introduction to Greek Epic Poetry	17
3)	An Overview	37
4)	Textual Analysis	41
	Books 1-4	41
	Books 5-8	59
	Books 9-13	75
	Books 14-18	96
	Books 19-24	114
5)	Structural Analysis	134
6)	Essay Questions and Answers	154
7)	Annotated Bibliography for the Odyssey	159

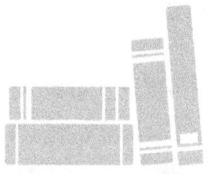

INTRODUCTION TO HOMER

Andra moi ennepe, Mousa, polytropon, hos mala polla plagchthe, epei Troies hieron ptoliethron eperse

O Muse, tell me about the man, you know, the crafty one, who was hounded for so long after destroying the holy city of Troy.

With these words opens one of the two greatest **epics** by the best epic poet. Homer wrote the *Odyssey* to tell the story of one man who lived vicariously for all men. It is no accident that the first word of the **epic** is andra, man. The **epic** is not about gods, or God, or to justify His ways to man. The **epic** is about man, whom the Greeks knew for certain to be "the measure of all things."

However distant Homer is from us, we can without the slightest effort transport ourselves into the life he describes. And we are thus transported chiefly because, however alien to us may be the events Homer describes, he believes in what he says and speaks seriously of what he is describing, and therefore he never exaggerates and the sense of measure never deserts him. And therefore it happens that, not to speak of the wonderfully distinct, lifelike, and excellent characters of Achilles, Hector, Priam, Odysseus, and the eternally touching scenes of Hector's farewell, of Priam's embassy, of the return of Odysseus, and so forth, the whole of the *Iliad* and still more of the *Odyssey*, is as naturally close to us all as if we had lived and were now living among gods and heroes.

(From Leo Tolstoy, "Homer and Shakespeare," in *Recollections and Essays*, translated by Aylmer Maude. Oxford: Oxford University Press, 1937).

But not all literary creatures, including friendly literary creatures, feel the *Odyssey* is good art. T. E. Shaw, better known as Lawrence of Arabia, translated the *Odyssey*, I conjecture, because he believed he was a type of Odysseus, the wanderer and marvelous adventurer, but did not approve of it as great art:

Crafty, exquisite, homogeneous - whatever great art may be, these are not its attributes. In this tale every big situation is burked and the writing is soft. The shattered *Iliad* yet makes a masterpiece; while the *Odyssey* by its ease and interest remains the oldest book worth reading ... Gay, fine, and vivid it is ... Book XI, the Underworld, verges toward terribilita - yet runs instead to the seed of pathos, that feeblest mode of writing. The author misses his every chance of greatness, as must all his faithful translators.

(From "Translator's Note," *The Odyssey of Homer*, translated by T. E. Shaw. Oxford: Oxford University Press, 1932).

THE PRE-HOMERIC AGE

Early Settlers In Greece

By as early as 6500 B.C. nomad-farmers had crossed over the Bosporus into Europe and settled in northern Greece. Some other farmers followed the Danube into central Europe. Those who had settled in northern Greece and Macedonia moved slowly southward in Greece into Thessaly and built primitive settlements at places like Sesklo and Dhimini. Unfortified houses here were erected with brick walls on stone foundations, and their inhabitants were farmers who tilled local fields and worshipped big-breasted, fat-thighed female fertility goddesses. By 5000 B.C. culturally related farmers who raised sheep, pigs, and cattle had settled in Crete and particularly in Knossos. Settlers moved to the Cyclades, islands between Greece and the Asia Minor coast, by 4000 B.C., and onto the Greek mainland by 2800 B.C. This early island civilization moved ahead of the rest of Greece in developing copper tools and weapons, stone-cutting, pottery and jewelry working. Meanwhile in Egypt and in Asia Minor copper became the most sought-after war material; tin, its alloy in bronze, was also coveted. In Egypt and Sumer and Akkad the political leader with the bronze weapons invariably conquered his enemies and friends alike. Moving from east to west, these metals and their resultant weapons arrived first in the Cyclades, then in Greece proper.

Troy Is Founded

One of the many fortified sites that sprang up at this time (ca. 3000 B.C.) was Troy on the Scamander river on the Asia Minor side near the Hellespont. A vigorous people apparently founded this city and the surrounding farming and trading communities. In the city itself archaeologists have discovered one of the earliest megaron buildings, a long, narrow room with a portico at the front and a fireplace in the center of life. We see this type of building many centuries later in Mycenae in southern Greece. In Troy we find also a new type of black polished pottery different from what had preceded in this area and in Greece.

New Immigrants In Greece

For one reason or another, perhaps because of massive migrations of people all over what is now southern Russia and western Turkey, a new race of man, formerly called Aryans but now known by language instead of race as Indo-European speakers, came into the Aegean area. The new immigrants were a broad-skulled people, and they apparently settled both peacefully and in a warlike fashion with the earlier narrow-skulled, Mediterranean type people. One of the places settled was Mycenae, home of Homer's *Agamemnon*. These new "invaders" brought with them black polished pottery, some of it with geometric patterns painted on it, and also megaron-styled houses.

Minoan Civilization

To keep our chronology in something resembling order, we must break away at this point and move to Crete, the island between Greece and Africa. Because of its position as a crossroads for trade, Crete was a natural site for early development. Trade between Greece and Egypt and Greece and the East frequently stopped in Crete. The early civilization in Crete is known as "Minoan" after the mythical king Minos who ruled his labyrinth kingdom at Knossos. The famous archaeologist Sir Arthur Evans gave it that name. By 2300 B.C. there was a flourishing civilization on Crete, which created marvelous painted vases, gold jewelry, faience ornaments, and carefully carved ivory pieces. The farmers on Crete were already cultivating olive groves. About the beginning of the second millennium B.C., the individualistic units scattered around Crete began a rapid process of urbanization with Knossos, Mallia, and Phaestos leading the way. An early model of the famous palace of King Minos at Knossos probably dates back to this time, as well as the beginning of crowded cities, roads for commerce, and hieroglyphic writing from Egypt which apparently evolved into what we now call Linear A. Though the Cretans had a knowledge of bronze swords, they did not seem to have made them in great numbers, or to have fortified their cities with walls. It is clear that by the year 2000 B.C. Cretan civilization surpassed any other on the Greek mainland or on the islands

Arrival Of Homer's "Achaeans"

Then after 2000 B.C. a very special event took place, of particular importance to our study of Homer, the immigration into Greece of Greek-speaking peoples, or the evolution of a very early form of Greek, which was not as yet set out in what we recognize as the Greek alphabet. This early form of Greek clearly belongs to that vast group of languages known as the Indo-European family which includes Latin and Romance languages, Germanic, and Sanskrit. The language of the early native inhabitants of Greece was not Greek, as can be discerned from place names like Corinth and Cynthos, which predate the invaders of 2000 B.C. and are not Greek, linguistically speaking. The invaders, who were inferior culturally and learned much from the Mediterranean aborigines, moved down from the north (i.e., the plains of southern Russia), and their grave sites reveal that they had domesticated both cattle and horses. The age of 2000-1500 B.C., known as the Middle Helladic (Early Helladic 3000-2000 B.C.), saw a southward movement of these proto-Greeks into the Greek mainland and the growth of cities at Mycenae and Tiryns in the Peloponnesus. Those proto-Greeks brought with them (as their trademark almost) a gray (yellow in south Greece) pottery called "Minyan" ware. It replaced the brighter preceding pottery. It is these proto-Greeks who brought the Greek language into the Aegean basin. Later Homer would call them "Achaeans," and still later archaeologists would refer to them as Mycenaeans. The ancient Greeks called themselves and their first ancestors Hellenes. These Hellenes roamed throughout Greece and settled the land by force, by farming it, by stealing it, and by killing off the earlier inhabitants. What had begun in 2000 B.C. was concluded by 1500 B.C.: the Hellenes were in control of Greece. The most powerful city-state in Greece was Mycenae "rich in gold," as Homer says, ruled perhaps by an early ancestor of Agamemnon, "lord of hosts and ruler of Mycenae."

FALL OF CRETE: RISE OF MYCENAE

While Mycenae prospered from 2000 to 1500 B.C., so did Crete, particularly Knossos, its chief city, whose magnificent ruins have been restored by Sir Arthur Evans (at his own expense!). Even by present standards Knossos would be large and prosperous. The local economy was based on agriculture and trade which extended to Egypt, Syria, mainland Greece, and southern Italy. The Mycenaeans traded with the Cretans and prospered. The gold from the Mycenaean graves and the money spent on the massive beehive tombs are accurate indicators of the wealth of Mycenae.

History In A Myth

It is necessary to emphasize that the Cretans and the Hellenes were not the same people, and while in 1500 B.C. they traded, they were not subjects one to the other. Mycenae and its allied cities or city-states ruled the Greek peninsula; Knossos and its allied cities ruled the sea and the sea trade. A conflict was surely inevitable. The Mycenaeans were (generally speaking) a Western race, Cretans an Eastern people. The former were taller, had the square northern skull; they had horses and chariots pulled by horses. The Cretans had a matriarchal religion in which they worshipped the earth-mother; the Mycenaeans a patriarchal system in which they worshipped the sky-god. According to mythology (which here may be more truth than fiction), one of the great rulers at Knossos was Minos whose wife Pasiphae conceived a bestial lust for a great bull, from which union was born the Minotaur. According to ancient tradition the Minotaur was housed in a huge labyrinth and every year tribute in the form of young (and virginal) men and women was offered to the bull-man in his labyrinth. This tribute was exacted from the city of Athens, until Theseus, the son of the king, went to Knossos as part of that tribute and slew the Minotaur. So much is myth, or more exactly legend, behind which probably lies some historical reality. Following the suggestions of many others, we would like to support the belief that behind the legend lies the historical expansion of the Achaeans or Mycenaeans from Greece into Crete and the capture of that island and its capital, Knossos. The Minotaur in the labyrinth is then explained as the king, Minos, whose symbol of power and royalty was the bull, in the labyrinth of his palace in Knossos. A brief glance at the plans and reconstruction of this palace (Paul MacKendrick, *The Greek Stones Speak.* New York: St. Martin's, 1962, pp. 46-52; 93-117) will illustrate even to an obtuse observer how impressed must have been the people of Greece at the splendor, size, intricacy, winding passages, and artwork of Minos' palace. It is little wonder then that visitors returning to Mycenae or Athens from Knossos spoke of the king's labyrinth. A visitor from Georgia would have a similar reaction to the Pentagon.

Knossos Destroyed

The imminent conflict and struggle between what we have called the Mycenaeans or Achaeans (Greeks) and the Minoans

(Cretans) apparently came to a head around 1400 B.C. Minoan civilization reached its zenith for about one hundred years on either side of 1500 B.C. Then in 1400 B.C. Knossos was destroyed in a terrible fire. Some say the destruction of Knossos was due to an earthquake; others that an earth-shaking volcanic explosion on the island of Thera, which was stronger than the 1883 volcanic eruption of the island of Krakatoa, destroyed Knossos and many other Cretan cities (an interesting sidelight here is the observation that the cities destroyed in this hypothetical holocaust were looted, and whoever heard of a looting volcano?); still others believe that the Mycenaeans, a raiding race of people who later raided Troy, according to Homer, methodically overran the island, destroying and looting.

The plot of our little mystery thickens when we add to it the appearance of what are called Linear B tablets. These tablets, deciphered in the 1950s by the young British architect Michael Ventris (who taught himself Greek in six weeks) as an early form of Greek written in a syllabic script (i.e., ka instead of two separate letters k + a) turned the scholarly world upside down for a time. Sir Arthur Evans, the great man of archaeology in Crete, had proposed a theory of Cretan dominance of the Greek mainland, which was contradicted by the decipherment of the tablets and the tablets themselves. If the tablets were Greek (i.e., Greek language) and Evans himself had found many tablets in Crete, his hypothesis of Cretan influence is then exactly opposite to the facts: the Mycenaeans, after learning from and trading with the Cretans, launched a military campaign against the same Cretans around the year 1400 B.C. and forced the island to become a Mycenaean satellite. But Evans refused to believe any of the new evidence or new theories. The arguments about the "Linear B problem" or the "Minoan Problem" came to be one of the biggest scandals in the scholarship of the ancient world (scandals among classicists, it must be remembered, are academic and force no government to resign), and evolved to the sad state of affairs in which certain archaeologists, who had acquired immense popularity with the Greek government, were able to keep other archaeologists from working in limited areas of Greece and from uncovering new evidence. The controversy continues to the present date.

Mycenaean Trade With Troy

All argumentative theories aside, the decline and destruction (or vice versa) of Knossos opened the road for the advance of the Mycenaeans. The demise of the Minoans left a vacuum which the Achaeans filled quickly, as they spread their influence throughout the Aegean world. They moved into Cyprus (for copper), Rhodes, Asia Minor, Syria, and westward to Sicily. At each center of Mycenaean power palaces grew up (Tiryns and Mycenae). A megaron, with a porch of pillars at one end and an overall oblong shape with a central hearth and above it an open roof, was the center of attraction in every palace. The wealth and power of the "lord of hosts" at Mycenae are well illustrated by the tholoi in which the kings were buried. The tholos tomb or "beehive tomb" has the shape of a cone, built with consummate skill out of cut stone. These tombs were dug into the sides of the hills and approached by a monumental entrance. Once Mycenaean governors had taken over Crete, it again flourished, and we can see the Mycenaeans trading even with Troy (Troy VI, as the archaeologists would have it, 1700-1300 B.C.), a future enemy.

Homer's Mycenaeans

The world which Homer describes in the *Odyssey* should be the world we have just been looking at, the Aegean world of

1184 B.C., the traditional date for the fall of Troy to the Greeks. But Homer's **epics** are oral epics and in the course of telling and retelling are altered by contemporary events, until they reflect better the society that succeeded the Mycenaean civilization and immediately preceded Homer's age (800 B.C.). The society and life described by Homer are surely a composite picture of the Mycenaeans and their successors from 1400 to 800 B.C. Archaeologists have established 1250 B.C. as the date for the fall of Troy; 1184 B.C is the traditional date. It is surprising to see how accurate tradition can be.

From Homer we learn that Agamemnon, as the most powerful leader among the Mycenaeans, requested all the Greek or Achaean princes to send aid to help in the war against Troy. From the remote area of the West and Ithaca came Odysseus, who owed a certain allegiance to Agamemnon. In the *Iliad* Homer tells of the Greek siege of Troy, in the *Odyssey* of Odysseus' journey back to Ithaca twenty years later. But Homer does not tell us that the war against Troy was really a form of organized piracy, that the Mycenaeans or Achaeans were in actuality sea-raiders (a polite word for pirates), and that they (principally) were responsible for destroying all sea trade in the Aegean and eastern Mediterranean. Piracy and trade have never mixed well. As the strength in military terms of Mycenae and her allies grew, so did the piracy. There are Hittite and Egyptian records which record the name "Achaeans" in extant inscriptions, and these records surely prove connections with the Mycenaeans. From these and other Hittite and Egyptian documents and from Mycenaean sources, we can speculatively conclude that there was a fairly high level of competition for trade between the Mycenaeans, Hittites, and Egyptians, and that the raiding parties of the Mycenaeans enriched the Greeks momentarily but destroyed a previously profitable (to all concerned) trading industry. These are the Mycenaeans sung about by Homer, but they have been romanticized in the interval from 1200 to 800 B.C., and are no longer pirates but heroes. It is interesting to observe that both pirates and heroes obey no national law and are free from the constraints and restraints of a society based on order. Greek heroes obey only the law of inner direction. With time, then, the pirates are transformed into heroes; the worshippers of Homer and Greek patriots made them Greek legends.

Dorian Invasion

Exhausted by constant warfare, around 1200 B.C. the Hittite kingdom collapsed and disappeared, the power of Egypt was destroyed, never to rise to great heights again, and then the might of Mycenae gave way. The Bronze Age of the Mediterranean world was now tired and fell of its own weight and also before the onslaught of a new and warlike migration of Greeks who entered the Aegean world about 1100-1000 B.C. This was an uncivilized race of men who destroyed the much higher, civilized nations who had migrated to Greece before them. The new wave of Greeks are called Dorians, and they plunged the ancient world into a dark age such as it would not see again until the Roman Empire disintegrated. The impact of the Dorians on the Bronze Age world was so severe that until 750 - 700 B.C. no written records were made. The Dorians had caused the Greeks to forget how to write - and we know that they had been writing since at least 1400 B.C. The Dorians were a blight and scourge on the land. They were also mighty warriors and with them came iron swords and iron implements of war into the Aegean world. The shock was terrible and the Greeks themselves did not recover from it until 800 - 750 B.C. when writing and Homer came upon the scene.

LIFE DURING THE TROJAN WAR

Economy During Mycenaean Times

During the period of the Trojan War, Greece was broken up into many small kingdoms, with a social and economic system similar to that of Europe in the Middle Ages. The main economic unit was the oikos, or house. Surrounding the oikos was enough farm and pasture land to support the oikos-owner, his family, and his servants and slaves. The servants had various functions to perform, such as herding the pigs, goats, and cattle kept by all oikoi (the plural of oikos). They also had duties to perform about the house. Most of the slaves in any household were women, since it was general practice among the victorious Greeks to kill all the men they conquered and capture the women for slavery. These female slaves helped the mistress of the house in weaving, washing, and nursing. Few of the servants and slaves had specialized skills. The minstrels, carpenters, metal-workers, physicians, and prophets formed a class by themselves. They were not attached to any one house, but went wherever their services were needed. Thus, each oikos was a nearly self-sufficient unit and was independent of every other oikos, although the oikos-owner did owe allegiance to the king of his land. As a result the household-owners and their families formed an aristocracy. Everyone else, whatever his or her position, slave or free, formed the masses.

It was only during a war that the household-owners acted together. The wars they engaged in were probably not fought for the acquisition of land, but rather to gain metals, precious or otherwise. Some people think that the Greeks warred with Troy to gain their iron. The Greeks themselves saw no difference between a war and a pirate raid. Indeed, Odysseus saw nothing wrong with interrupting his journey home to sack the city of Ismarus, taking all the booty and wives his crew could carry (Bk. 9).

Assemblies

During peacetime, the only official place for the nobles to meet was at the assembly, which was convened by the king. These assemblies were called by the king whenever he had an important decision to make concerning all the nobles (that is, the oikos-owners) in his land. Although he had the power to make decisions without consulting them, he rarely did so. At an assembly the nobles would discuss the problem before them, judging it on the basis of their local traditions. It is no wonder that Homer considered the assembly a vital part of any civilized society. For example, when he describes the barbaric Cyclopes (Bk. 9), Homer is quick to point out that they have no assemblies and live without traditions. On the other hand, the Phaeacians (Bks. 6, 7, 8), whom Homer considers to be over-civilized, are constantly having assemblies.

Guests And Hosts

In a world where contact among nobles living in the same country was usually limited to infrequent assemblies, contact among nobles living in different countries was a rarity. There was no king and no law to regulate such "international" affairs. Instead, people had to depend on each other's good will. From this dependence, an elaborate tradition developed concerning the relationship between travelers and their hosts. For example, hosts were expected to protect their guests from harm. Thus,

Theoclymenus approaches Telemachus and openly admits to having killed a man. He is now escaping from the dead man's relatives and asks Telemachus if he can sail with him. Telemachus permits Theoclymenus to sail with him and invites him to Ithaca, where he will be safe.

Of course, the guest had responsibilities to his host. The traditional cause of the Trojan War was a breach of faith on the part of a guest. Paris (also called Alexander), who was a guest in the house of Menelaus, seduced Menelaus' wife, Helen, and ran away with her to his native city, Troy.

Gifts

In a society where there is no money, trade (or barter) usually becomes the accepted method of transferring goods. This is what happened in Greece in Homeric times. The barter system developed within the rules of the guest-host relationship, where all actions were considered to be between friends, even though the two people may never have met before. It is not surprising, therefore, that objects given in trade were always considered to be gifts. Throughout the *Odyssey* people give gifts. But it must be remembered that the person giving a gift expected to receive a gift in return, even if he had to wait several years for it. This expectation of a gift in return for one already given is expressed by Laertes, Odysseus' father (Bk. 24). Odysseus takes advantage of the fact that Laertes doesn't recognize him after nineteen years. He lies to his father, telling him that he had seen Odysseus some years ago and had given him many gifts. Laertes tells this stranger (Odysseus) that he gave his gifts in vain, for now his son is dead and can no longer greet him with hospitality and gifts in return for those received (note how Laertes associates gift-giving and hospitality).

Trojan Archaeology

Let us now return to the subject of Troy. Schliemann, the first to excavate the site, recognized that there had been more than one city built on the same location. In fact, nine levels, indicating nine different towns, were observed. It remained for later archaeologists to make further refinements in the number of levels and to decide which of the levels was the Troy of the Trojan War.

Since any fortress built on this site is able to control all shipping traffic through the Dardanelles (the waterway leading from the Aegean Sea to the Euxine Sea), the site has been occupied almost continuously up to the present time. The first settlement was founded about 3200 B.C., in the Early Bronze Age. It started out quite small, increased its fortifications, and finally was completely destroyed by fire.

The second level, Troy II, was built on the ruins of Troy I after the fire. It too expanded as it grew more prosperous, and it too was destroyed by fire. Troy II was followed, logically enough, by Troys III, IV, and V. Each of these levels lasted about a hundred years and was inhabited by the same race of people.

Troy VI

The next level, built about 1900 B.C. and designated by archaeologists as Troy VI, was built by a new people. The evidence for this can be found in the remains of their buildings and their pottery, which differ in many ways from the work of the previous levels. What is most interesting about these new Trojans is that they were closely related to the Greeks. They were part of the same movement of people that had started in Central Europe and had spread out in all directions. One piece of evidence for this close relationship between the Trojans and the Greeks is the pottery remains found in Troy VI. This pottery was made with a certain technique that was used only by the Greeks of Mycenae. The possibility that these pots were imported from Mycenae (Mycenae at this time was carrying on trade throughout the Aegean Sea) is rejected because only the technique of manufacture is the same, not the styles. This technique is sufficiently complicated to rule out the possibility that the people of Mycenae and Troy developed it independently of one another. The only possibility remaining is that both groups learned it from the same source, their ancestors, and that these ancestors were the same for both Troy and Greece. In addition to the pottery technique, another link between Troy and Greece is the horse. The Greeks were the first to bring the horse to the Greek mainland, and there are no traces of horses in Troy before Troy VI.

Troy VIIa

Troy VI was destroyed by an earthquake in 1275 B.C. The next level, designated as Troy VIIa, was built soon after the destruction of level VI, apparently by the same people. There are several facts about the remains of this level which are of great interest to us. First, all of the houses had huge storage jars, as if the citizens needed to store great supplies of food during a siege; second, the town was destroyed by fire, the usual fate of a conquered city; third, two skeletons were found lying out in the open looking as if they had been killed; fourth, Troy VIIa was inhabited during the time that Greek historians, working without the aid of archaeology, said the Trojan War was fought. The probable date for the destruction of Troy VIIa is 1250, the very date given for the Trojan War by Herodotus, a Greek historian of the fifth century B.C. It is certain, therefore, that if there ever was a Trojan War, this is where and when it was fought.

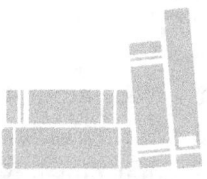

INTRODUCTION TO GREEK EPIC POETRY

GREECE AFTER THE TROJAN WAR

From the preceding sections, it is easy to see that scholars have a great deal of information about the social and historical background of the *Iliad* and the *Odyssey*. But if we ask about Greece 400 years after the Trojan War, we are on less sure ground. The Trojan War was fought about a century before the influx of Dorian Greeks to the mainland. These Dorians spread out over western Greece, bringing about the end of the oikos system of government. They left Greece without an alphabet, for the knowledge of writing Linear B was lost with the destruction by the Dorians of the major towns. For a period of about 400 years (1150-750 B.C.) until writing was reintroduced, there was no body of written literature in Greece. But this is not to say that there was no poetry being composed. Poems were composed to be recited orally.

COMMUNITY SPIRIT IN MAINLAND GREECE

The type of poem that was composed depended on the society in which it was produced. The Dorians were a communal people. That is, they lived and worked together, with very little conflict among individuals. It was this community spirit which produced the Spartans, the foremost of the Dorians in the fifth and fourth centuries B.C. The poetry that developed from such a society, mostly choral songs, aptly reflected the communal feelings of its inhabitants. These poems were not only sung by groups of people, but they frequently exalted the very group spirit that gave rise to choral songs.

INDIVIDUALITY IN IONIA

In the eastern part of the Greek-speaking world and on the coast of Asia Minor, as well as on the islands of the Aegean, lived the Ionian Greeks. Many of these Ionians were living in towns founded by Mycenae during the period of expansion and trade. Here, trade was still carried on with Egypt and with other lands.

Instead of the community spirit that evolved in the west, a sense of individuality was maintained throughout Ionia (as the Aegean Islands and the coast of Asia Minor are called). Quite naturally, the poetry of Ionia reflected this individuality. Instead of poems sung by many people, as among the Dorians, in Ionia the poems were recited by one person; and, what is more significant, instead of poems about the communal spirit, the poems of Ionia exalted the spirit of the individual. The two long poems we have from this period, the *Iliad* and the *Odyssey*, praise individual accomplishments

THE EPIC

One of the first questions to arise concerning the *Iliad* and the *Odyssey* is how, since there was no writing, anyone could memorize a poem the length of either of these two **epics** (about 350 pages in most books). It is generally true that in societies where there is no writing, people's memories are better than are the memories of people living in literate societies. Even today there are poets in Yugoslavia capable of reciting from memory poems the length of the *Odyssey*.

But good memory is not the whole answer. The minstrel, a bard who recited the poem, was expected to vary the story, however slightly, each time he recited it. Only recently have scholars understood how a bard was able to compose and recite his poem. Before we can learn the answer to this question we must first learn what a Greek **epic** is.

EPIC METER

An **epic** is a long poem, each line of which is in the same meter. The meter of the *Iliad* and the *Odyssey* (and, because of their great influence, all subsequent epics) is **dactylic** hexameter. "Dactylic" means that the basic unit of each line is in the form - v v, where - represents a metrically long syllable, v a short syllable (it is called **dactylic** because it is like our finger, one long joint followed by two short ones-dactylic is Greek for "finger-like"). "Hexameter" tells us that six of these dactyls make up a line. In practice, one or more of the dactyls (-v v) may be replaced by a spondee (- -), and the last foot is always a spondee. The feet of the **epic** may be represented thus:

-v v| - v v| - v v| - v v| - v v|- -

Some lines may be mostly dactyls-for example, the first line of the *Odyssey*:

andra moi ennepe, Mousa, polytropon, hos mala polla,

-v v| - v v| - v v| - vv | - v v| -

Some may have many spondees, as, for example, line 1 of Book 5 of the *Odyssey*:

Eos d'ek lecheon par' agauou Tithonoio, - -| - vv | - v v| - -| - -|-

In practice, the poet seems to have thought not in terms of feet (dactyls and spondees), but in terms of metrical limbs, or cola. That is, he thought of the line as a unit containing four, less often three, separate limbs. A full discussion of this aspect of **epic** poetry would go beyond the scope of this introduction. See the article by Howard Porter mentioned in the bibliography.

Of course, not all words can fit into this metrical scheme. For example, the combination - v - has no place in a **dactylic** line. Being barred from using certain words, the poet had to keep in mind, as he recited, a metrically proper word for each concept he might be called upon to use. Even a word that fits the **dactylic** meter cannot be placed anywhere in the line, but only where it fits. The poet had to remember not only the proper word but also the positions in the line where it could fit. This led to the poet's remembering whole phrases and, later, whole lines to express an oft-repeated thought. For example, the clause "when early-rising rosy-fingered dawn appeared" is, in Greek, one line of **dactylic** hexameter.

ORAL TRADITION AND THE FORMULA

These useful words, phrases, and lines were passed down from poet to poet until, by Homer's time (about 750 B.C.) it was possible to compose a long epic of great complexity and originality that was made up largely of formulas (as these standard words, phrases, and lines are called). It is thought that some of these formulas date back to the Trojan War itself and were handed down intact from generation to generation, even though the meaning of some of the words was lost. For example, Hermes is frequently called argeiphontes. Some people translate this as "the slayer of Argus," others as "brightly-appearing." Over a period of centuries, more and more phrases were retained in the collective memory of the minstrels, thus increasing the store of formulas. By Homer's time, every common word appeared in a number of formulas. The Greeks used the word "ship," for example, in the phrases "balanced ship" (2 feet), "dark-prowed ship" (3 1/4 feet), and "curved ship" (2 1/2 feet). These three formulas fit at the end of the line. Thus, as the singer recites the first part of the line, he plans ahead to have the end of the line 2, 2 1/2 or 3 1/4 feet long, so that he can fit in one of the "ship" formulas.

HOW INDIVIDUAL POETS COMPOSED

In this case, where a relatively common word like "ship" is involved, the poet rarely cares whether he calls the ship balanced, dark-prowed, or curved. Unfortunately, many people make the serious mistake of assuming that this is always so - that the poet always does not care what formula he uses as long as it fills out the line. These people have been especially critical of Homer's method of applying adjectives to names (epithets). In other words, what they are telling us is this: "As you read the *Odyssey*, and search for its meaning, ignore the epithets, for they do not mean anything. Homer put them in, these metrically convenient adjectives, because they fill out the line." As an example of their thinking, let us use the name Odysseus. If Homer wants to end the line with the word Odysseus, he has several adjectives to go with the name. Thus, if he has 2 feet left (- v v | - -), he will write dios Odysseus (divine Odysseus); if he has 2 1/2 feet left (v v | - vv | - -), he will write polymetis Odysseus (crafty Odysseus); if he has 3 1/4 feet left (v | -v v |-v v |- -), he will write polytlas dios Odysseus (much-suffering divine Odysseus). The people who maintain that these epithets have no meaning are led astray by the way they phrase the problem. It is true, they say, that, given a set number of feet at the end of the line and a name to go with this number, there is (usually) only one adjective that goes with this name to fill out the line. Therefore, they conclude, these adjectives are chosen solely for metrical convenience.

This would be true if their hypothesis were true - but it is not. The poet is not "given" a set number of feet to fill up with a name and an adjective. He controls the first half of the line as much as the last half. He decides whether there will be 2, 2 1/2, 3 1/4, or any other number of feet left over, and therefore he can decide in advance exactly which epithet he will use.

THE TEXT

Homer, the author of the *Iliad* and the *Odyssey*, lived at the time when the alphabet of the Phoenician traders was being adapted to the Greek language. He had the opportunity to do what none of his predecessors could have done-put his poems in writing. As the use of writing spread throughout Greece, so did the poems of Homer. Any Greek child who learned to read, learned to read Homer. Greeks prided themselves on knowing by heart long passages from the *Iliad* and *Odyssey*. Greek authors quoted Homer whenever they could, much as present-day authors quote the Bible and Shakespeare. Of course, there was no printing in those days so that each copy of Homer had to be written separately by scribes. It was only natural that mistakes crept into many of these copies. Since papyrus, the material made from an Egyptian plant upon which all texts were written, decomposed after a period of time, new copies were always being made. As a result, widely differing copies of Homer were circulated.

ALEXANDRIAN SCHOLARS

The situation would have become intolerable had it not been for the efforts of a group of scholars in Alexandria in the third century B.C. There, under the rule of Ptolemy I, a library was founded for the purpose of collecting as many texts as possible of all the Greek authors. When the copies of Homer were examined, it was discovered that they disagreed in many places. Lines that were present in some manuscripts were lacking in others. In some manuscripts, **episodes** were expanded. Three scholars associated with the Alexandrian Library, Zenodotus, Aristarchus, and Aristophanes (not to be confused with the famous fifth-century B.C. Greek comic playwright), worked to produce a standard text of Homer. In addition to working on the text, Aristarchus produced a commentary on Homer which dealt with a number of critical points. Many other commentaries were written, ranging from complete works to idle jottings in the margin of the text.

When parchment was developed, Homer's works, along with those of many other Greek authors, were transferred to this more durable substance. He was copied and recopied throughout the Middle Ages.

OTHER EPICS

The *Iliad* and the *Odyssey* are only two of many **epics** that were recited before the introduction of writing to Greece. Of the others, only two have come down complete. These are *The Works and Days* and *The Theogony*, both attributed to Hesiod. Unlike the heroic **epics** of Homer, *The Works and Days* is **didactic**; that is, it has something to teach. In this poem Hesiod (who, unlike Homer, speaks in the first person) lists the work that should be done on a farm and the best days to do this work (hence the title). In *The Theogony*, Hesiod presents, probably for the first time, a genealogy of all the Greek gods, starting with the first, Chaos, and ending with the minor gods. Of interest to us is the fact that he mentions two children born to Calypso and Odysseus (see Bk. 5 of the *Odyssey*).

The *Iliad* and the *Odyssey* are but two stories that revolve about the long Trojan War. We know of other **epics** that fill out the story from the judgment of Paris to the tale of Telegonus, a song of Odysseus. Our main source for these **epics** is Proclus, a grammarian of the second century A.D., who summarized their plots in his Chrestomathy. These stories form the Epic Cycle and are as follows:

1. *Cypria* (named after Cypris, another name for Aphrodite). This poem starts with Paris' decision that Aphrodite is more beautiful than either Hera or Athena. As a reward, Aphrodite, goddess of love, helps Paris to seduce Helen, wife of Menelaus. Paris and Helen escape to Troy. Menelaus and his brother Agamemnon marshal troops from nearly every Greek city. Odysseus, however, has no wish to fight for Helen's return. When the brothers come to enroll him in their cause against Paris and Troy, Odysseus pretends madness. Palamedes, a friend

of Agamemnon, suspects a trick and, taking Odysseus' infant son Telemachus, says that he will punish him. Odysseus stops his mad tricks at this point, as only a sane man would. Thus, the first draft-dodger was foiled. Later, Odysseus, with the aid of his friend Diomedes, revenges himself upon Palamedes by causing his death on a fishing trip. The events of the *Cypria* are carried up to the point where the *Iliad* begins.

2. *Iliad*. The *Iliad* revolves about Achilles, the mightiest of the Greek warriors. He withdrew from the battle after he was insulted by Agamemnon, who took away his mistress. It is only after the death of his best friend, Patroclus, at the hands of the Trojan enemy, that Achilles returns to do battle and kills Hector, the chief defender of Troy. Odysseus is the same daring and crafty person we see in the *Odyssey*. Although he objected to going to Troy, once there he devoted himself to its utter defeat.

3. *Aethiopis*, by Arctinus of Miletus. The action of the Trojan War is here continued up to the death of Achilles. Odysseus and Aias, another Greek warrior, fight over Achilles' armor.

4. *Little Iliad*, by Lesches of Mitylene. In this **epic**, Achilles' armor is awarded to Odysseus. Aias goes mad and commits suicide (when Odysseus meets Aias' ghost in Bk. 11 of the *Odyssey*, Aias, remembering this quarrel, refuses to speak with him). Odysseus then disguises himself as a beggar so that he may enter Troy undetected and plot with Helen for the downfall of Troy (this **episode** is told by Helen in Bk. 4 of the *Odyssey*). This **epic** ends with the Trojans taking the wooden horse into Troy.

5. *Sack of Troy*, by Arctinus of Miletus. The trick of the wooden horse succeeds. Troy is taken, and the long war ends. Odysseus kills Hector's son Astyanax by hurling him from the city wall.

6. *Returns*, by Agias of Troezen. This **epic** relates the return home of all the major Greek generals, except Odysseus, whose return is thoroughly detailed, of course, in the *Odyssey*.

7. *Odyssey*. This is the story of Odysseus' voyage home.

8. *Telegony*, by Eugammon of Cyrene. This is a zany continuation of the *Odyssey*, wherein Odysseus has many adventures and even marries again, although Penelope is still living. Telegonus, his son by Circe (see *Odyssey*, Bk. 10), comes to Ithaca to look for Odysseus and unwittingly kills him. Telegonus, discovering that he has killed his father, takes Penelope and Telemachus to Circe's island, where Telegonus marries Penelope and Telemachus marries Circe.

HOMER THE MAN

"Seven cities claimed the Homer dead/In which the living Homer begged his bread"

The coming of the Dorians on their raiding parties and in their colonization caused a number of mainland Greeks to leave their homeland and move to the islands off Asia Minor or to the Asia Minor mainland itself. It is here then in Asia Minor, which the Greeks called Ionia, that **epic** began. We do not possess **epics** earlier than Homer's, i.e., we do not have examples extant of the **epic** at its beginning. When we come across the epics of the *Iliad* and the *Odyssey*, they are already in a perfected literary state. Some less developed form surely preceded them-unless we are to believe that the **epic** was born fully grown like Athena from the head of Zeus. Without trying to escape from or run away from the problems surrounding the person of Homer, let it suffice us to say that sometime between 850 and 750 B.C. the greatest epic poet ever was born. If he did not write the *Iliad* and *Odyssey*, we must assume then that another man with the same name did. We may assume that he was born in Ionia, probably either in Smyrna or on the island of Chios. Five other localities also claimed Homer as a son: Rhodes, Colophon, Salamis, Argos, and Athens. There is also a tradition that Homer was blind, which may have been an accurate remembrance of things past. But in antiquity there was also a strong tradition that poets were seers and that, because of their divine gifts of seeing into the future, they were frequently blind, i.e., not able to see the present. Homer may have fallen into that class. Another explanation for the tradition is a fanciful etymology of the word Homer, ho-me-horon, the Greek for "one who does not see."

Homer stands at the end and at the beginning of a long tradition of epic poetry and wandering singers. He stands at the end of a tradition of oral poetry which had flourished in Greece for at least several centuries before him, but his written form of an oral **epic** is the only one to survive the ravages of time. He stands at the beginning of a tradition of Greek excellence in literature and intellectual curiosity which refused to die until suppressed by the Christian church. It is surely stressing the obvious, but it cannot be repeated too often for the sake of the uninitiated, to say that the Greeks are a nation of storytellers. Homer is the earliest extant example of such Greek storytellers, but he is definitely not the absolute earliest. In their simplest form the *Iliad* and *Odyssey* are songs about heroes, and in each of these songs we find mention made of other songs (i.e., epics) and other singers. We thus have **epics** within epics.

In the *Iliad* the hero like Achilles (Bk. 9.186) and the heroine like Helen (6.357) sing about themselves or imagine themselves as the subjects for song in the years to come. In the *Odyssey* we are at a later date when singers had become professional, paid entertainers. (We believe that Homer set the *Iliad* down in verse as a young man, and the *Odyssey* as a mature man.) We see that the profession of a singer or rhapsode is easily as esteemed as that of a physician (*Odyssey* 17.381 ff.). Demodocus, a blind singer (shades of Homer!), is asked to perform at the Phaeacian court (8.44) where he is given a seat of honor. He recites his stories to the accompaniment of a lyre and the dancing of young people. In this eighth book of the *Odyssey* Demodocus chooses as his song the struggles and events around Troy-all the while Odysseus is in his audience! Odysseus sits down and, hearing a song about himself (it is almost like a modern news broadcast-here it is an oral **epic** within a written epic), is moved to tears.

HOMER: A TYPE OF POET

As we can see from the *Odyssey* itself, wandering singers are part of the social life of the Mycenaean world (Homer's dramatic date) or of the Greek world in the 9th-8th centuries (Homer's date). In addition to Demodocus we see a singer named Phemius entertaining the suitors in Odysseus' house. According to the best of contemporary scholarship, it is believed that Homer is a type of singer, "a singer of tales", much like Demodocus and Phemius, and probably one of the last in the long tradition of **epic** singers; for Homer, or his scribe, seems to have written down the *Odyssey* on some material, and in so doing to have separated himself from a long line of singers.

The great sea raids of the Mycenaean people in the Aegean Sea from 1500 B.C. to the coming of the Dorians in 1000 B.C. or so was also an age of heroes and the first awakenings of national pride. Among these peoples it was beginning to be important to be Greek as opposed to Trojan. Agamemnon called together all his vassals, i.e., all Greeks, for the great national campaign (i.e., sea raid) against the Trojans. It was obviously very important in this aristocrat-dominated society to have a lofty reputation and image. The traveling singer of tales provided both an articulation of this new awakening of nationalistic aspirations and also an organ for propaganda of the aristocratic families and their famous members. Within more historically chronicled times, we see Pindar (518-438 B.C.) singing the praises of various aristocratic individuals who have won laurels in athletic contests. These singers of tales come forward for our recognition as early as the later Mycenaean age (1200 B.C.), but surely were in existence for some years previously. As we can see from the *Odyssey*, these early singers recited at the courts of aristocrats and were highly regarded. As concerns their artistic material, it seems that they had a vast store of memorized materials which, when called upon, they would reproduce for the occasion. These singers clearly had excellent memories and committed to them thousands and thousands of lines of verse. It appears that these singers could, upon request, recite long poems or **episodes** from what we later have designated as epics. Or, at very formal occasions and with some forewarning, they could recite through long hours and over the span of several days a whole **epic** of the proportions of the *Odyssey*. Such performances were usually held at religious and state functions. Such poets were considered highly skilled craftsmen.

These early singers did not have a written text which they committed to memory. Rather they learned their material from other singers. Perhaps this skill was passed on in a guild or from father to son. Whatever the method, these singers developed incredible memories, a thing necessitated by the absence of writing. (Plato warned that writing would destroy memory and understanding-if he could only see the present xerox-generation!) But they did not memorize verbatim; they memorized plots, scenes, and speeches, but allowed themselves room for improvisation. Thus no two performances of an **epic** were identical in every part. They actually composed as they sang-we now call it oral composition. This oral composition or improvisation was aided by the use of formulae. A formula is a stock adjective or phrase which is repeated over and over, to join scenes, to set the stage, to change speakers, and to describe regular occurrences. Many days begin with the formula: "rosy-fingered dawn ..." Small formulae could be expanded into large, typical, and repeated scenes: assemblies of the army; funeral rites; scenes of games; arming for the battle. Each scene of a game is a formula if it is similar to other scenes of games. Most are alike.

The poet only knows one basic type or pattern for a game scene. Throughout the **epic** he gives merely variations of the motif. Add to all this the fact that the minstrel has a personal and intimate familiarity with the story, and we should not be surprised at a poet who can recite an **epic** of 10,000 lines.

Through the pace-setting work of three men, Albert Lord, Mathias Murko, and Milman Parry, evidence has been brought to the attention of the literate world that there are South Slavic **epics** being sung from memory, at the present in the Serbo-Croat region, which bear a strong resemblance to the *Iliad* and the *Odyssey* in method of composition and type of plot. All these South Slavic texts have been taped and stored at Harvard.

At some point in history, probably between 800 and 750 B.C., one of these minstrels, who sang of Achilles and Odysseus, material he had learned from his predecessors, met a man who had learned from his predecessors to read and more importantly to write. The poet sang and the scribe copied the texts which later became the *Iliad* and the *Odyssey*. The above is apocryphal-only in detail, not in thrust.

HOMER'S CRITICAL REPUTATION

To speak of **epics** is to speak of Homer. They constitute an equation: Homer = **epic**. This condition has prevailed since the sixth century B.C., when Homer was enthroned as the supreme poet and philosopher. The *Iliad* and *Odyssey* were the only Bibles. Homer had said everything worth saying, and everything he said was operative in and for all times. Homer stands at the beginning of the awakening or renaissance of Greek intellectual life as well as of literary life. The student studying this period is well advised to read Bruno Snell, *The Discovery of the Mind* (1953). Homer provides our first real look at the early Greek intellect, religious life, and social structure, which all, of course, were already in an advanced stage of development. Homer transmits for us, as he did for his Greek audience in the succeeding centuries, a view of the Mycenaean world, the first truly Greek world. He is the only connecting link between the Mycenaean world and the later Greek world across a bridge of dark centuries from 1100-800 B.C. Homer may in fact be more than a bridge for the later Greeks to approach their ancestors. It appears that he is the interpreter of the Greeks for the Greeks. Whatever the pattern of life, Homer sets it. As an example: in the area of religion Nilsson, in his book *Homer and Mycenae* (1933), assembles the evidence to show that the concept of the Greek system of deities, a group of twelve deities headed by Zeus and living on Mount Olympus, is really a reflection or remembrance by the Greeks of the Mycenaean royal houses. This image is preserved only by Homer in the *Iliad* and *Odyssey*. The great Olympian deity Zeus is in reality Agamemnon, king of kings; and the lesser Greek kings are the lesser Olympians. Euhemerus, a fourth-third century B.C. philosopher, expounded such a theory when he claimed that all gods were originally humans who were deified after death.

HOMER AMONG THE ROMANS

The critical reputation of Homer did not decrease when the Greek world became the Roman Empire. No one, except for Lucan, the Latin **epic** writer of *Pharsalia*, thought of writing an **epic** unless it sounded like Homer's epics. Vergil is a virtual slave to Homer. The *Aeneid* Bks. 1-6 is patterned after the *Odyssey* and Bks. 7-12 after the *Iliad*. Homer's critical reputation remained strong; he was always admired. But his influence waned as a knowledge of Greek in the West died out with the coming of the Dark Ages; Latin epics, especially those of Vergil and Statius, became dominant.

HOMER AND THE ROMANTICS

The Renaissance brought about a revival of Classical scholarship and interest in ancient literature, but this generally applied only to Latin literature because of the continual lack of Greek teachers or readers. It did not take long, however, for critical opinion to turn to Homer. He was a favorite of the romantics and was popular in England and on the continent - especially with Goethe (1749-1832) who at the age of twenty-one began to teach himself to read Homer in Greek! The romantics were particularly attracted to Homer who represented to them a naive and simple-minded poet, who stood for a type of noble savage. Such a view was set forward in some detail by Robert Wood in *An Essay on the Original Genius of Homer* (1769). This is not a critical work in the contemporary sense of the word; it is more like a gentleman's essay on the subject.

"HOMERIC QUESTION"

The first critical work of serious scholarship on Homer was the *Prolegomena ad Homerum* by Friedrich Wolf in 1795. He sought to prove that Homer could not have composed the *Iliad* and *Odyssey* because at the time of Homer's death, writing had not yet been developed in Greece. Wolf opened a can of worms which has not been closed since. The discussion about who Homer might have been and whether or not he wrote the *Iliad* and the *Odyssey* has now been institutionalized, and is known around the world in scholarly circles as the "Homeric Question." This quarrel is concerned generally with these points: Did he write both works or one only? Are the stories basically fact or fiction? Was the author of one or both **epics** a mere compiler of popular sagas?

The two sides in this battle are called "the unitarians" and "the separatists" (analysts). The names are self-explanatory. The unitarians have enjoyed the favor of most scholars; they are the conservatives and have the authority of ancient opinion to support them. The separatists, who deny that one man wrote both **epics** or even all the parts of one epic, are the more ingenious, and also the minority. Their hero is Friedrich Wolf. A typical argument of the separatists against the unitarians goes something like this: We believe that one man did not write the *Iliad* but rather gathered together a group of stories and compiled them into a rather clumsily constructed epic; the "joints" of these various stories show where the compiler sewed them together; for instance, in *Iliad* 5.576 we learn that Palaemenes has been killed but later in 13.658 we see him lamenting his dead son. A single author would not have made such a mistake.

Great classical scholars like Karl Lachmann and A. Kirchhoff joined the ranks of the analysts. Even the greatest classicist, Wilamowitz, believed in a kind of "cut and paste" job for Homer's **epic**, in which the poet borrowed his entire **epic** from stories already in existence. We can add to this list of separatists the name of Denys Page, Regis Professor of Greek at Cambridge, who in *History and the Homeric Iliad* and *The Homeric Odyssey* has become one of the leading contemporary spokesman for those who believe in the multiple authorship of the *Iliad* and *Odyssey*. In the ranks of the unitarians we can see Sir Maurice Bowra (*Homer and his Forerunners* and *Tradition and Design in the Iliad*) and Wolfgang Schadewaldt *(Iliastudien and Von Homers Welt und Werk)*.

Much of the effort of scholars working on Homer in the second half of the twentieth century revolves around oral poetry, oral composition of epics, and analysis of such literary devices as formulae. The impetus for these studies was effected by Mathias Murko, Milman Parry, and Albert Lord.

EXEGESIS OF HOMER

Students interested in working through a detailed analysis line by line of the 20,000-plus lines of Homer and also interested in any one of thousands of particular problems of a literary, archaeological, anthropological or sociological nature, would do well to consult Wace's and Stubbing's "handbook" entitled *A Companion to Homer*. They have developed no particular critical approach to Homer, but they have assembled enough data to help any student or scholar develop his own approach. Added to such pieces of high scholarship we can also see silly books and critical approaches like those of J. A. Scott in his *The Unity of Homer*, whose motto obviously was "damn the evidence-straight ahead for unity." Professor J. L. Myres, an archaeologist, thought of Homer's works as a source book for ancient history and archaeology, and he proceeded "to mine" them. Denys Page sees the *Iliad* in the same light. It is amazing how many scholars can analyze a work of art, but treat it like a cadaver under examination by a group of pathologists. It is a sad day in which literary pathologists determine the nature and structure of criticism. But all is not gloom. The student with fine literary sensitivities will be richly rewarded by reading Homer with S.E. Bassett through the medium of his book *The Poetry of Homer*.

WAS HOMER A WOMAN?

Our critical view of Homer, particularly of his *Odyssey*, has been broadened and sensitized by a group of scholars who have dealt with the epic from the feminine psychological point of view. Because of the minor role given to women in the *Odyssey* this approach may at first appear ridiculous. But what if a woman had written the *Odyssey*? An examination of the **epic** with that in the background would prove, at least, interesting. In 1897 Samuel Butler, better known as the author of *The Way of All Flesh*, produced a study called *The Authoress of the Odyssey*, in which he claimed, perhaps as a pretext only for his in-depth study, that Nausikaa, the jeune fille of Bk. 9 of the *Odyssey*, had written the *Odyssey*. To the conservative classical establishment this must have appeared the silliest of books. Too many classicists of yesterday and today have written and continue to write books on works at art without recognizing the difference in analysis and criticism between a work of art and a work of non-art. Criticism should point out the difference. The analysis of a plant and that of an **epic** should be different. In addition to identifying folk tales and their use by the author of the *Odyssey*, Butler makes a strong case for the author's perceptiveness of the menacing quality and strength of individual females, e.g. Circe, and the Sirens. To a certain extent even Penelope is a threatening character. Starting from this background, G. E. Dimock, in the Spring 1963 issue of the *Hudson Review*, delves into the menacing quality of Odysseus' actions and feelings, trying to decide what type of man Odysseus is, a man who can survive the death of so many friends and then calmly trap a house full of guests and servants and kill them.

The critical reputation of Homer and his *Odyssey* is bright and farreaching. The music and the poetry of the *Odyssey* receive a considerable amount of scholarly attention and verbiage. The dispute over the importance of oral composition and its effect or influence on this **epic** attract at present the best minds in classical circles. A small group persists in mining the *Odyssey* for historical data.

THE ODYSSEY

AN OVERVIEW

BOOK 1

The first book informs the reader of the imprisonment of Odysseus on Calypso's island, Ogygia, in the tenth year after the Trojan War. It also describes the insolence of the young nobles in Ithaca (led by Antinous and Eurymachus) who, in the absence of Odysseus, live off his wealth and woo his wife, Penelope. After the invocation to the Muses, with which the *Odyssey* opens, a council of the gods is summoned, during which Zeus decides that Odysseus shall return home safely and Athena shows herself to be the champion of Odysseus. The goddess visits Telemachus, son of Odysseus, in disguise, gives him courage to rebuke the suitors, and persuades him to seek news of his father by sailing to the mainland. The suitors retire to their homes and Telemachus goes to bed.

BOOK 2

On the next day, which occupies Bk. 2, Telemachus calls the first assembly of the Ithacans since the departure of Odysseus for

Troy. Telemachus formally upbraids the suitors, demanding that they quit the palace and leave his mother to her grief. Antinous retorts that the suitors will remain until Penelope weds one of them and he denounces Penelope's ruse. (She had vowed to choose a husband when she completed a shroud she had been weaving for Laertes [Odysseus' father]. But each night she unraveled the portion she had woven during the day.) A pair of eagles is interpreted as a favorable omen by Halitherses, a seer, and Telemachus requests a ship for his voyage. After Telemachus dissolves the assembly, the goddess Athena, disguised as Mentor, a faithful lord, promises to procure a ship and crew. At the palace, after an exchange with Telemachus, the suitors grow worried about his plans. Telemachus enjoins Eurycleia, nurse of Odysseus, to prepare provisions in utter secrecy; he then departs at night and sails until dawn.

BOOK 3

On the morning of the third day, Telemachus arrives in Pylos, kingdom of aged Nestor, who had fought in the Trojan War. Telemachus and his guide Athena, still in the form of Mentor, are welcomed by the Pylians, who are sacrificing a bull to Poseidon, god of the sea. Telemachus identifies himself and announces his mission. Nestor's reply is characteristically lengthy: he reports the homecoming of the heroes of Troy, relating the murder of Agamemnon by his wife, Clytemnestra, and his cousin, Aegisthus, and the revenge of Agamemnon's son, Orestes, who slew the murderers of his father; Agamemnon's brother, Menelaus, was unable to intervene, for unfavorable winds had carried him to Egypt. Nestor bids Telemachus visit Menelaus at Sparta and offers him, on Athena's suggestion, a chariot and his son, Peisistratus, as companion. Telemachus spends the night at Nestor's palace and, after a sacrifice, travels throughout the fourth day and part of the fifth to Sparta.

BOOK 4

In the evening of the fifth day, they arrive at Menelaus' palace, where his daughter's wedding is in progress. Menelaus is amazingly wealthy but unhappy over the fates of the heroes of Troy. His wife, Helen, recognizes Telemachus by his resemblance to Odysseus and pours a potion into the wine to ease the grief of all. She tells a story about Odysseus in Troy; Menelaus answers with a tale of Odysseus' cunning while in the wooden horse. The next morning Menelaus tells how Eidothea, a sea-nymph, daughter of the sea-god Proteus, helped him escape the island of Pharos, where he was stranded: in seal-skins for disguise, following her instructions, Menelaus and his men trapped and held fast Proteus, who could assume any shape. Proteus was forced to tell Menelaus his destiny, with information about other heroes, including Agamemnon and Odysseus.

Back at Ithaca, the suitors learn of Telemachus' trip and plan an ambush at the island of Samos. Penelope hears of their plot, but Athena in a dream assures her of her son's return.

BOOK 5

Bk. 5 opens on the seventh day of the poem with a second council of the gods on Olympus, whence Hermes, messenger of the gods, is dispatched to Ogygia to order Calypso to release Odysseus. Calypso, reluctantly agreeing, seeks out Odysseus, who sits weeping on the beach. She instructs him to build a raft.

This he completes in the next four days; the day following, he departs for Phaeacia. On the eighteenth day of his voyage (the twenty-ninth day of the poem), he spies Phaeacia, but Poseidon, returning from Ethiopia, in anger sends a storm against him and wrecks his craft. Then he swims for two days and nights upon a divine veil received from the sea-nymph Ino until he reaches the coast. Odysseus escapes the sharp crags with a prayer to the gods and falls asleep beneath the brush on the shore.

BOOK 6

Before the dawn of the thirty-second day (this book and the next), Athena visits Nausikaa, princess of Phaeacia, and in a dream instructs her to wash her clothing when the day breaks, lest a marriageable girl be dressed unseemly. So in the morning she goes to the river where Odysseus is asleep. With her attendant maids she tosses a ball, and the girls' screams awaken Odysseus. Naked and unkempt, he beseeches her pity in a careful, flattering speech. Persuaded, she offers clothing and oil with which to wash. Odysseus reappears, exceedingly handsome, and wins from her a description of the city (for it would be improper for her to accompany a stranger into town), with the advice to pass by Alcinous, the king, and to clasp the knees of her mother, the queen, in supplication.

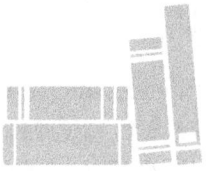

THE ODYSSEY

TEXTUAL ANALYSIS

BOOKS 1-4

BOOK 1

The first ten lines of the poem contain an invocation to the muse of epic poetry. Homer pretends that the muse is speaking through him. Compare this to the bard Phemius' statement (Bk. 22, 347): "I am self-taught; a god caused all sorts of song to be in me." Phemius and Homer see no contradiction in crediting their self-taught skill to the gods. Homer, in this invocation, is really asking that his memory not fail him.

Comment

The opening word of the *Odyssey* is andra "man", who for Homer is the "measure of all things." He invokes the Muse to help him, or to speak through him. Vergil imitates these opening lines, and the pattern is thus set for all time; in **epic** the Muse is regularly invoked. Compare the opening lines of Milton's *Paradise Lost*:

Of Man's first Disobedience, and the Fruit Of that Forbidden Tree, whose mortal taste Brought Death into the World, and all our woe ... Sing Heav'nly Muse ... That to the heighth of this great Argument I may assert Eternal Providence, And Justify the ways of God to men.

This latter piece is surely Christian, full of missionary intent, but the Muse is invoked to spread the kingdom of God! The poet sings of man, the sinful being. The andra of line 1 is Odysseus who is called polytropus "crafty". He is not a saintly man; he is an adventurer. This sets the mood for the entire *Odyssey*. We are to be treated to an adventure story. Later Milton treats us to fire and brimstone.

After the invocation we learn of Odysseus' present condition. He alone of all the Greek chieftains who fought in Troy has not yet reached home because he has angered Poseidon, the god of the sea. Ten years have passed since the fall of Troy, but Odysseus is still far from Ithaca. At present, he is being held by the nymph Calypso on the island of Ogygia.

Comment

We must ask ourselves why Homer chose this particular place to start his story. Odysseus is not at the lowest point in his travels. He is on a mythical island, Ogygia, whose name came to mean "primitive". In addition, the name of his captor, Calypso, means "concealer". The *Odyssey* traces Odysseus' journey from unreal Ogygia to Ithaca, very much a part of the real world. Odysseus, the hero, had left Ithaca twenty years earlier, fought at Troy for ten years, and then spent ten more years on his return journey to Ithaca. He left Ithaca a great hero and returns an even greater one. The name of Odysseus is known now all over the Mycenaean world. His journeys added fame to his cult and depth and understanding to his character. Odysseus follows exactly the outline identified by Joseph Campbell, in his *The Hero with a Thousand Faces*, as the route for all heroes:

The standard path of the mythological adventure of the hero is a magnification of the formula represented in the rites of passage: separation-initiation-return: which might be named the nuclear unit of the monomyth. A hero ventures forth from the world of common day into a region of supernatural wonder: fabulous forces are there encountered and a decisive victory is won: the hero comes back from this mysterious adventure with the power to bestow boons on his fellow man.

The gods now hold a meeting on Mount Olympus. Athena, Odysseus' patron among the gods, takes advantage of Poseidon's absence to bring up the topic of Odysseus' wanderings. Perhaps, she thinks, now that Poseidon, who hates Odysseus so much, is away, she can bring about Odysseus' safe return.

Comment

In her plea in behalf of Odysseus, Athena makes a punning reference to Odysseus' name. When she asks why Zeus hurts Odysseus so much, she uses the verb odyssomai, "to cause pain to." The Greeks took these accidental similarities very seriously. Later on, especially in Bk. 19, Odysseus will be further implicated with the word odyssomai and the notions of giving and receiving pain.

Zeus blames all of Odysseus' troubles on his brother, Poseidon, who became angry when Odysseus blinded his son,

Polyphemus. This story will be related in Bk. 9. Zeus, however, has no definite plan to suggest, perhaps fearing his brother's wrath. But Athena presses her advantage and suggests a scheme that Zeus cannot refuse - that Hermes, the messenger of the gods, be sent to tell Calypso to release Odysseus and that she herself go to Ithaca in order to raise the spirits of Odysseus' son, Telemachus, and to send him to Pylos so that he might get news of his father.

Athena now carries out her half of the plan. She, like all the gods, has the power of assuming various shapes. Here she makes herself look like a pirate chieftain, Mentes. She enters the main hall where Telemachus and the suitors for the hand of Penelope are seated.

Comment

Notice the way in which we are introduced to the suitors. They are eating Odysseus' food and forcing his servants to wait on them. They are also sitting on the hides of cattle which they themselves had killed. By this act they make themselves equals in sin to Odysseus' companions, who slaughtered the cattle of the Sun (Bk. 13). As we proceed, we will see other ways in which Odysseus' companions and Penelope's suitors are similar. But are the gods any better than the suitors who are eating up his estate? They interfere with and harm Odysseus more than any suitor. Homeric gods are totally anthropomorphized.

The suitors ignore Mentes (Athena); only Telemachus greets her and, as was the custom, offers her food before asking her any questions about herself. While they are eating, Phemius, the minstrel, sings for all the diners.

> **Comment**

Homer is quick to defend his fellow minstrel by pointing out that Phemius is forced to play for the suitors. Minstrels regularly made the rounds of wealthy homes and performed at their parties. At such occasions, minstrels were given preferential treatment and special honors.

In response to Telemachus' worried questions, Athena encourages him by reminding him of his father's craftiness and ability to get out of tight places. She then asks him who these people are who are eating another person's food so greedily. Athena, of course, knows who the suitors are, but this gives Homer an excuse for telling his listeners (remember that Homer was a bard just like Phemius) all about the suitors. We learn that all the men of Ithaca who were too young to journey to Troy have now grown up and are all courting Odysseus' wife.

> **Comment**

It seems that all of Odysseus' wealth stays with Penelope, so that Telemachus will get none of it should she marry one of the suitors. Property apparently follows a matrilinear progression in Ithaca, and this fact reflects the old civilizations of Greece, perhaps Mycenaean, but more likely the Eastern civilization that preceded the Mycenaeans.

Athena urges Telemachus to call an assembly of the suitors for the next day and at the meeting to tell them to go to their own homes. She also, as she had told Zeus she would, suggests that he leave Ithaca to seek news of his father; first to Pylos,

Nestor's kingdom, then to Sparta, the home of Menelaus and Helen. Athena reminds him of Orestes, who avenged his father's death.

Comment

Briefly, the story of Orestes is as follows: Agamemnon, Orestes' father, who was leader of the Greek forces in Troy, was slain upon his return home by his wife, Clytemnestra, and his cousin, Aegisthus, who were living together as man and wife. Orestes, aided by his sister, Electra, slew Aegisthus and his mother. (The stories of the murder of Agamemnon and of Clytemnestra and Aegisthus are told in the *Agamemnon* and *The Libation Bearers* by Aeschylus.) The story of Agamemnon's murder is mentioned several times throughout the poem (we even meet his ghost in Bk. 11) and is obviously meant to contrast with the story of Odysseus. In the one case, we have a king who returns home quickly only to meet his death; in the other, a king who makes his way home only after troubles and travels, but succeeds in regaining his rightful position. The contrast between the two wives is even more striking: Clytemnestra is the murderess of her husband; Penelope waits nineteen years for her husband's return although she is not even sure he is still alive.

As Athena takes her leave of Telemachus, the young man offers her a gift, as was customary in Homeric times. Athena, being a goddess, refuses the gift and leaves. We now return to Phemius, who has been singing all this time. He is reciting the tales of the Greek warriors. This brings Penelope down from her chambers to scold Phemius for reminding her of her long lost husband. Telemachus, however, defends Phemius' right to sing about whatever he thinks will be popular. Telemachus finishes by saying that he is the master of the house-a statement that surprises his mother, who is used to thinking of Telemachus as a young and irresponsible boy. Telemachus also takes advantage of the fact that he is now the center of attention to order the suitors' to attend an assembly the next day. Now it is the suitor's turn to be amazed at this new Telemachus who is ordering people about. He is answered curtly by Antinous and Eurymachus, the spokesmen for the suitors.

After much dancing and singing, the men leave the hall to go home. Telemachus goes to his bedroom. accompanied by his faithful nurse, Eurycleia.

Comment

Homer tells us as much about Eurycleia as he would about a brave hero. This is Homer's way of stressing her importance. Just how important she is we will see in Bk. 19 and following. Eurycleia had earlier been Odysseus' nurse and was apparently an old family servant. The men in Greek families were brought up by their nurses, and in Telemachus' case his nurse is personally more important than his mother. Penelope seems to represent for Telemachus only an access to his father's property and kingship.

BOOK 2

Book 2 starts at dawn of the next day. Telemachus dresses and orders his heralds to call the men of Ithaca to assembly. From Aegyptius, one of the old men, we learn that this is the first assembly to be held in Ithaca since Odysseus left to go to Troy.

BRIGHT NOTES STUDY GUIDE

Comment

The mood of this book is set by the first page. Telemachus is taking up his father's role in Ithaca: "he sat in his father's seat and the old men yielded to him." The elders would not have been so respectful if they thought him still a child. While Telemachus is gaining a new awareness, Ithaca is regaining an old awareness in holding its assembly. Assemblies, where all the male citizens gather to discuss and decide upon matters of policy, are, for Homer, the mark of a civilized people. When, for example, Homer wants to characterize the race of the Cyclopes as primitive, he says that they have no "counselbearing assemblies" (Bks. 9, 112), or when he wants to describe the over-civilized Phaeacians, (Bks. 7, 8), he shows them constantly holding assemblies.

Telemachus delivers a moving speech, listing all the injustices and misfortunes that have befallen him and his household: not only is his father gone (and presumed dead), but the younger lords are consuming his livestock and are behaving intolerably. Towards the end of his speech, with great passion, Telemachus begs the intruders to leave his household alone. As he finishes the speech, he bursts into tears. Antinous, seeing that the assembly is taking pity on Telemachus, tries to place the blame on Penelope. Penelope, he says, had promised the suitors that she would marry one of them. She had declared that she would choose a husband as soon as she finished weaving a funeral shroud for her father-in-law, Laertes. But, Antinous complains, she had unraveled at night what she had woven during the day and was thus able to keep them waiting for over three years, until they discovered her trickery and forced her to finish the job. Antinous suggests that Telemachus give his mother in marriage to whomever her father, Icarius, might choose. The suitors will not leave until she marries one of them.

Telemachus rejects Antinous' suggestion and repeats his command that the suitors leave. Two eagles are seen and interpreted by Halitherses, a seer, as a favorable omen sent by Zeus. Halitherses had predicted that Odysseus would be away for nineteen years; now in the nineteenth year, he predicts death for all the suitors. Eurymachus scolds Halitherses for encouraging Telemachus and echoes Antinous' threat that the suitors will stay until Penelope chooses one to be her husband. Telemachus, of course, rejects Eurymachus' demand as he had rejected Antinous'. He now asks for a ship and twenty men (twenty being the usual number of men on a boat in peacetime) so that he might sail to Sparta and Pylos in search of news of his father. If he should learn that Odysseus is dead, he will give his mother in marriage to one of the suitors.

Now one of the older men present, Mentor, rises to speak. He blames the other old men for allowing the disgraceful conduct of the suitors to continue. When Odysseus was home they were all treated justly and kindly, yet now they are doing nothing to repay the kindness. As it was meant to, this statement provokes the suitors. Leiocritus speaks for the suitors saying that it would be foolish for the old men to fight over a "dinner" since even Odysseus could not drive them out if they were not willing.

The elders, who were probably disturbed by Mentor's suggestion that they fight the suitors, quickly leave to go to their homes. The suitors also leave the assembly, but they go to Odysseus' house to consume more of his food.

Comment

By telling us that the suitors returned to Odysseus' house and by contrasting them with the law-abiding elders who went to their own homes, Homer dramatically reinforces what we already know - that the first of the two purposes of the assembly has failed. Telemachus has not convinced the suitors to leave; he is not yet his father's son in every way. Telemachus is learning what it means to grow up in the shadow of a famous father, to compete with one of the greatest of Greek heroes, and to lose. Telemachus is intent, however, on searching out the location of his father and escorting him home - not out of love for his father but because his father's name and also his own are dirtied by the stain of inaction. His family is losing face, a loss not permitted to heroes.

After the assembly breaks up, Telemachus goes to the seashore where he can be alone. There he prays to Athena, who comes to him in the guise of Mentor. She praises him for his conduct during the debate, telling him to forget the suitors for the present and to prepare for his journey.

Comment

Whether we regard Athena as an actual goddess appearing before Telemachus or as a manifestation of Telemachus' unconscious, she dispels his sadness at having failed in his first public demonstration of his manhood. Athena is the protectress of the city, of law and order, and as such she protects the proper order of things, i.e., Odysseus' house belongs to Telemachus. The movement of deities between heaven and earth shows the anthropomorphic conception of Greek deities. Xenophanes, the Greek philosopher, noted that if Greek animals were to make gods, they would all look like animals.

Telemachus, thus encouraged by Athena, cuts short his moping and returns home. There he refuses to sit and dine with the suitors as he had been accustomed to doing. He ignores the two suitors who taunt and mock him. He leaves the main hall and asks Eurycleia to prepare wine and food for his journey. The faithful nurse warns him that the suitors will start plotting against him as soon as he is gone and that he had better stay home and guard his property. Telemachus insists that he must go and swears Eurycleia to secrecy.

Athena again disguises herself as a human, this time as Telemachus himself, and picks out the twenty men for the crew, instructing them to be ready by evening. She then causes the suitors to fall into a heavy sleep. Appearing once more in Mentor's form, she tells Telemachus that the ship is ready. Telemachus and his men leave Ithaca under cover of darkness and sail through the night.

BOOK 3

Book 3, like Book 2, starts at daybreak: Telemachus and his crew arrive at Pylos, the first stop in his quest for information about his father. As they arrive, the Pylians are on the beach sacrificing eighty-one black bulls to Poseidon, the sea god and enemy of Odysseus. Athena, who has accompanied Telemachus, gently reproaches him for being the last to leave the ship.

As soon as Nestor, king of the Pylians, sees Athena and Telemachus approaching, he greets them. His son Peisistratus offers the intestines of a bull and some wine to Athena, so that she may continue the prayers to Poseidon. She asks that she and Telemachus might accomplish their mission and then might return home safely.

Comment

As it turns out (Bk. 5), it is Athena herself, and not Poseidon (who could not care less), who makes sure that Telemachus arrives safely home. Also, notice that the Greeks (and most other ancient peoples) burned the inedible portions (bone, fat, etc.); the edible parts of the animals they saved for their own stomachs. The usual diet in Mycenaean times and down into that of Homer was meatless, except for some fish. More cattle were slaughtered by Homer in the *Iliad* and *Odyssey* than probably existed in all of Greece. It strikes the modern reader as peculiar that ancient deities chose sides in battles and, in addition, chose favorites for benefits and others for hatred. Each ancient individual had his own special deity, in much the same fashion as Roman Catholics have special saints.

Just as Telemachus did in Bk. 1, Nestor waits for his guests to finish dining before asking them their identities. This was so customary that, even though there was a fair chance that the visitors were pirates, Nestor waits for the end of the meal to find out who they are. Telemachus tells him who he is and asks him if he knows anything about Odysseus' fate.

Nestor's reply stretches over two pages, yet it nowhere provides an answer to Telemachus' question.

Comment

Nestor is the first minor character we meet who also appears in the *Iliad*. We immediately see that he is the same talkative old man who continually gives advice. His speech is a fine study of the way some old people speak. He lets memories of the Trojan War overwhelm him, and his speech becomes the earliest example of "stream of consciousness." He rambles from topic to topic, mentioning Odysseus' name a few times, but never giving any concrete information about himself, or even admitting that he does not have any information.

Nestor now asks Telemachus why he allows the suitors to consume his food and torment his mother. If Athena favors Telemachus, he says, as much as she did his father, then the suitors would soon be too bruised to think of eating or wooing. Nestor tries to keep up the hope that Odysseus is still alive. When Telemachus sounds pessimistic about this, Athena says that it is better to undergo many hardships to get home safely than to arrive home quickly only to be murdered by your wife, as happened to Agamemnon.

Telemachus uses this mention of Agamemnon as an excuse to ask Nestor about Agamemnon and Menelaus, Agamemnon's brother. Nestor, of course, is only too happy to be given the chance to tell a story. In addition to the tale of Agamemnon's death, Nestor relates the wanderings of Menelaus. Menelaus too, it seems, had traveled for many years before reaching home.

Since it is now nightfall. Athena suggests that they finish their sacrifices and go to bed. Telemachus and Athena start for the ship, but Nestor is unwilling to lose two such eager listeners. He invites them to stay at his house, and offers them aid in their journey to Sparta.

Athena begs off, giving the excuse that she must leave early in the morning. Why she bothers giving this excuse is a mystery, since she immediately changes into the shape of a vulture and flies away. Nestor interprets this metamorphosis as meaning that Athena favors and is watching over Telemachus.

Nestor and Telemachus now go to the palace, where a bed is prepared for Telemachus. The next day, Nestor calls together all his sons and announces that he will pay homage to Athena by offering her the gilded horns of a young cow.

After Nestor's commands are carried out, Telemachus and Peisistratus leave Pylos. The journey takes two days. They spend the first night at the house of Diocles, in Pherae. By traveling all the next day, they reach Sparta, Menelaus' city, by nightfall.

BOOK 4

Telemachus and Peisistratus arrive at Sparta just as Menelaus is celebrating the coming marriage of two of his children-a daughter who will marry Neoptolemus, the son of Achilles; and a son, Megapenthes, who will marry a local Spartan girl. The two travelers are told to wait while an attendant asks Menelaus whether they are to be invited in or sent away. Menelaus demands that they be brought in immediately to share in the feast. As they are eating, Telemachus points out to Peisistratus the precious metals and amber which decorate Menelaus' palace. Although Menelaus is quick to disclaim any rivalry with Zeus, he nevertheless has no doubts that he is the wealthiest man in the world.

Comment

Menelaus, like Agamemnon, is presented to us for comparison with Odysseus. His great wealth is the first example of his current happiness. Though he is involved in the blood feud between Atreus, his father, and Thyestes, his uncle, he is spared any troubles, all of which are transferred to his brother Agamemnon. Menelaus and Helen spend eternity in Elysium. Menelaus and Agamemnon serve as types of Greek heroes who returned from Troy. Agamemnon came home to Mycenae immediately after the war and was promptly murdered by his wife. Menelaus returned to Sparta and was blessed by the gods. Odysseus was not allowed to return home.

As Menelaus speaks, he mentions (and praises) Odysseus. Hearing his father's name, Telemachus breaks into tears, just as Helen, Menelaus' wife, enters the room with her attendants. Characteristically, Helen recognizes at once who Telemachus is, although she has never seen him before.

Comment

This one action by Helen does more to establish her character than any objective description could ever do. Homer, like most literary artists, prefers to let the character's actions and words speak for themselves. For example, the magnitude of Helen's beauty is expressed, not by Homer's narrative, but by the reaction of the elders of Troy as they see her approaching (*Iliad* 3, 154-158).

They all exchange gossip and revive painful memories. They become so sad that Helen pours a pain-relieving drug, an ancient tranquilizer, into their drinks. Now that the men are in a gayer mood, Helen narrates one of Odysseus' exploits in the Trojan War. Odysseus, she says, disguised himself as a beggar and sneaked into Troy in order to familiarized himself with the town. Helen, of course, saw through his disguise. Odysseus, having reconnoitered the town, slew some Trojans and escaped back to the Greek camp.

Menelaus too has a story to tell about Odysseus. When the Greek warriors were hidden in the Trojan horse, Helen, who had learned of the plan from Odysseus, approached the horse and whispered to the men inside, assuming, in turn, the voices of several of their wives. Some of the men inside the horse were taken in by this impersonation and would have leapt out, thereby giving away the Greeks' scheme, had not Odysseus held them back.

After these two anecdotes, they retire for the night. The next morning, Telemachus tells Menelaus the purpose of his visit and asks him whether or not he has any news of Odysseus.

In answer, Menelaus tells of his stay in Egypt. He was forced to remain on a small island because there was no wind to drive his ship. After he was marooned for twenty days, the goddess Eidothea took pity on him. She was the daughter of the island's ruler, whose name was Proteus and who was called the Old Man of the Sea. Eidothea told Menelaus that if he could catch her father, Proteus, he would tell Menelaus which god was so angry at him that he was kept prisoner on the island. This was much easier said than done, for Proteus had the power of assuming any shape he wished-even fire or water. Eidothea helped Menelaus further by disguising him and three of his men in smelly sealskins so that they could sneak up on Proteus.

Menelaus did as Eidothea told him. When he had Proteus in his power, he asked him about his comrades who had fought with him at Troy. Proteus told him of two who died, Aias of Locris, and his own brother, Agamemnon. Aias was killed by Poseidon, the very god now so angry with Odysseus. Menelaus also learned of Odysseus - that he was being held by Calypso.

The above information had to be forced out of Proteus. He then offered something voluntary: Menelaus was not destined to die. The gods would send him to Elysian Fields where there is no snow or rainfall.

Comment

Proteus' prophecy that Menelaus will be taken to Elysium encourages his natural indolence and laziness, which earlier had allowed Paris to steal his wife Helen. It is this lack of energy and heroic qualities in Menelaus which Kazantzakis despised so much, and the abundance of which made Odysseus one of the most memorable of Greeks.

After finishing his story, Menelaus invites Telemachus to stay with him for another week or so and offers him three horses as a gift. Telemachus declines to accept the horses, offering the rockiness and grasslessness of Ithaca as an excuse. Menelaus then offers him a gold and silver mixing bowl, which Telemachus accepts.

The scene now shifts back to Odysseus' palace in Ithaca. The suitors find out that Telemachus has taken a ship to look for his father. They now fear what Telemachus may be planning on his return. Antinous suggests that they lie in wait and ambush him as he approaches Ithaca.

A herald, Medon, overhears this plot and at once goes to inform Penelope of it. Penelope is doubly shocked-first, at the plot itself; second, at the fact that Telemachus is not in Ithaca. Eurycleia, who is present, tells her about Telemachus' trip and advises her to pray to Athena for his safety. After she does this, Penelope goes to bed. Athena, in the guise of Penelope's sister, visits her to soothe her fears about Telemachus. She refuses, however, to dispel Penelope's fears about Odysseus.

As the book closes, the suitors establish their ambush and await Telemachus' homecoming.

Comment

The first four books of the *Odyssey* tell of Telemachus' growing up and his wanderings in search of Odysseus. For this reason, they are often referred to as the Telemachy. But they do more than merely describe Telemachus' actions at this time; they also set the scene for Odysseus' homecoming. Odysseus' presence is felt throughout the four books. By having all the action and dialogue center around Odysseus, Homer allows us to know exactly how all the characters (including such minor figures as the nurse Eurycleia and the bard Phemius) feel about Odysseus. Also, by giving us such a substantial picture (one-sixth of the poem) of the real world of Ithaca, Homer lets us have a firm basis for comparison with the fairyland world that Odysseus will be traveling through in the next seven books.

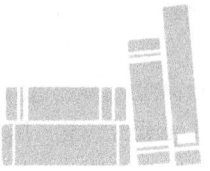

THE ODYSSEY

TEXTUAL ANALYSIS

BOOKS 5-8

BOOK 5

This book opens with a second meeting of the god, Athena reminds the gods of Odysseus' stay on Calypso's island. Zeus orders Hermes, the messenger of the gods, to hasten to Calypso and to order her to release Odysseus, who should travel to Scherie, where he will be given an escort home.

Comment

This second assembly seems to ignore the first. There too Athena brought Odysseus' present condition before the gods, and there she suggested that Hermes be sent to Ogygia to secure Odysseus' release. Homer's preference for duplication and his predilection for the simplistic in structure over the complicated, results in a very straight-forward and uninvolved plot. Homer is not fond of keeping two or three threads of a plot straight.

This same approach extends even to his grammar which is paratactical and not syntactical: e.g., Homer writes two or three simple sentences rather than one main sentence with two or three dependent clauses.

Hermes now carries out Zeus' request. He takes his magic wand, which has the power both the awaken people and put them to sleep, and travels through the air to Calypso's isle.

Comment

The island is described in somber, almost funereal terms. The trees are tall and stately; the birds are predatory and nocturnal. This is a suitable picture of a land ruled by an immortal goddess who has the power of bestowing immortality on humans. In the *Odyssey* as in the *Iliad* eternal life is equivalent to death. The goal of the hero is glorious life, not long life. Odysseus is luckier than most; his life is long and glorious. Life should involve struggle and the knowledge of one's own mortality, which is the meaning behind Socrates' gnothi sauton, "know thyself," i.e., knowledge that you are not a god.

Hermes enters Calypso's cave, but finds only the goddess present: Odysseus is sitting by the shore crying and grieving over his exile.

Comment

Notice Odysseus' utter passivity. Compare it with the last time we see him, at the very end of Bk. 24, where he is compared to an eagle swooping down on its prey.

Calypso reacts to Hermes' message as any woman would. Angrily, she curses the gods for interfering in the love affairs of goddesses. Now that she can no longer keep Odysseus, she suddenly no longer wants him. "Let him go, but I'm not going to help him in any way." Hermes, ignoring this last remark, repeats Zeus' demand that she send him on his way.

After Hermes leaves, Calypso approaches the weeping Odysseus. She tells him nothing of Zeus' role in his leaving, but presents the plan as her own. Odysseus is naturally suspicious of this sudden concern on Calypso's part and demands that she promise to do him no harm as he journeys homeward.

She agrees to this, but tries once more, as she must have tried many times in the last seven years, to convince Odysseus to give up his thoughts of home and stay with her as her immortal husband. Odysseus says that he is willing to risk death at sea, so strong is his desire to see his wife.

The next day Calypso gives him tools and points out the best trees for a raft. The journey on this raft is the first part (for us, the readers) of Odysseus' journey from the land of fairy tales to the real world. Homer stresses the importance of the raft by describing in detail its construction.

After four days of work, Odysseus finishes his raft. He sets off on the fifth day with supplies given to him by Calypso. He sails out into open water, out of sight of land, and so must guide himself by the sun and stars (in general, the Greeks sailed along the coast, never losing sight of land). On the eighteenth day, he comes in sight of Scherie, the home of the Phaeacians. But Poseidon, Odysseus' enemy, who is on his way back to Olympus after three weeks in Ethiopia, spies the raft. Enraged at Odysseus and angered by the gods who plotted against him in his absence, Poseidon whips up a fierce storm.

Comment

Homer says that Poseidon concealed the earth and the sea with a cover of clouds. The Greek word for "concealed", calypsai, has the same root as Calypso, whose name means concealer: an example of a Homeric play on words. We see here that by the grace of the gods Odysseus is freed by one concealer only to be re-concealed by the anger of another god. Poseidon, who had been on a three-week vacation, is indignant, more because the other deities acted against him, than because he hated Odysseus. Poseidon is a completely anthropomorphized god.

Odysseus, tossed about by the mountainous waves, is knocked from the raft. Weighted down by the clothes Calypso gave him, he barely manages to scramble back aboard.

Fortunately, there is a witness to Odysseus' plight. It is Leucothea, a goddess who was once a mortal. She was made a goddess after she leapt into the sea with her son in order to escape from her crazed husband. She takes pity on Odysseus and offers him her magic veil which will protect him as he swims toward Scherie. But Odysseus doesn't know whether to trust her (for all he knows, this storm was caused by Calypso, who broke her promise to him), and he stays clinging to the raft until a gigantic wave breaks it apart. This decides the issue: Odysseus dives into the sea and starts swimming. He swims for two days; at the dawn of the third day, he sees Scherie. His happiness dissipates however, when he approaches the shore. The coast is a rocky cliff and there are rocks along the shore. If he tries to land there, he will be cut to pieces by the pounding surf; despite his efforts, he is swept in towards the rocks by a breaker. He succeeds in clinging tightly to a projecting rock; as the wave rushes back towards the sea, it takes Odysseus with it, leaving pieces of his skin stuck to the rock.

Comment

This scene of one man battling the elements is unique in Greek literature (except for Philoctetes' battle with the island of Lemnos), which elsewhere deals with man as a social animal.

Odysseus is swept by the currents to the mouth of a river. Swimming up the river, he finally staggers onto the shore, swollen from his long swim in the sea. He unties Leucothea's veil from about his waist and tosses it back to the sea. Under a pair of olive trees growing around each other, Odysseus prepares a bed of leaves and quickly falls into a deep sleep.

BOOK 6

While Odysseus sleeps, Athena is preparing the way for his entrance into the city of the Phaeacians. This people had once lived in Hyperie, near the Cyclopes (the one-eyed giants encountered by Odysseus in Bk. 9). Rather than fight the Cyclopes, who were continually robbing them, the Phaeacians chose to emigrate to Scherie. There, far from any neighbors, they built houses and temples and apportioned the land for farming. Their current leader is Alcinous.

Athena now comes to Alcinous' daughter, Nausikaa (Naw-si-kay-a), in a dream, and puts the idea into her head to go to the river the next day in order to wash the family's dirty clothes (thus conveniently providing male clothing for Odysseus). Nobody, says Athena, wants to marry a girl who always has heaps of dirty laundry.

> **Comment**

Nausikaa is the typical princess of fairy tales. And, in many ways, Odysseus is the typical stranger who arrives in the princess' land, demonstrates his prowess, and (if this were a true fairy tale) marries the princess. Much of the dialogue in this book should be read with an awareness of how Homer is playing with the typical fairy tale and using it for his own ends.

Nausikaa heeds the dream (after all, no self-respecting princess in a fairy tale wants to hurt her chances of marriage) and asks her father for a wagon and mules to carry the clothes to the river. She says her reason for wanting to clean them is that she wants her father and her brothers to be well-dressed. But Alcinous is not deceived-he knows the real reason for her concern and grants her request.

> **Comment**

Epic similes differ from simple similes in that they are much more elaborate. The function of a **simile** is to illustrate. In Homer "similes perform two functions: they illustrate by providing a more or less exact working model of the original, and they have a compositional function of underlining a particular event either to show its importance ... or to relate it to other events by contrast or by echo" (Webster). Though the **epic** similes in the *Iliad* are more developed than those in the *Odyssey*, a good example is found in Book 6.102 ff: "When they had finished eating, the nubile girls together with the princess began to play ball; they threw off their outer cloaks and Nausikaa began to sing. Like Artemis, the archer, who runs down the mountains, along the ridges of high Taygetus or Erymanthus, amusing herself by chasing boars and swift deer, and wild nymphs following, the daughters of Zeus, and Leto is delighted, while above all she raises her head, and quickly she is recognized, though all are lovely; just so the virgin Nausikaa surpassed her friends in beauty." All of this is one **simile**; it did not die, however, with Homer. Compare this **epic simile** from Milton's *Paradise Lost*:

"Thus Satan talking to his nearest mate With head uplift above the wave, and eyes That sparking blazed; his other parts besides Prove on the flood, extended long and large Lay floating many a rood, in bulk as huge As whom the fables name of monstrous size, Titanian, or Earth-born, that warred on Jove, Briareas or Typhon, whom the den By ancient Tarsus held, or that sea beast Leviathan, which God of all his works Created hugest that swim the ocean stream ... So stretched out huge in length the Arch-Fiend lay."

Nausikaa and her maids take the clothes to the river and wash them in the running stream. After this work they are ready for a picnic and games while the clothes dry in the sun. Odysseus is all this while lying fast asleep under a bed of leaves near the spot where the merry party is playing. Nausikaa, too eager in her game, throws the ball out into the river. Seeing the ball drift away, the girls let out high-pitched shrieks, which awaken Odysseus. He, of course, has no idea where he is or who these shrieking girls are. Naked and salt-encrusted, he steps forth and appears suddenly before the girls, with just a leafy branch to conceal his nakedness. Homer compares him to a hungry lion in a herd of sheep or deer, and hungry he must certainly be, after three days in the sea without food.

Needless to say, the girls are quite surprised at the sight. All of them except Nausikaa scurry away. Odysseus debates with himself whether he should clasp her knees (the standard act of supplication) or stand at a distance and request some covering. He wisely chooses the latter course. Keeping a respectful distance between them, Odysseus gives an exceedingly tactful speech: he first compares her to the goddesses in beauty; he then congratulates her parents on having such a graceful daughter, but (he continues cleverly, knowing just as Athena did how a young girl's thoughts revolve around marriage) happiest of all is he who will be her husband. After giving her just enough information about himself to make her take pity on him, he returns to the subject of her marriage.

All this has the desired effect on Nausikaa: she offers him clothing and aid. She calls to her fleeing maids, ordering them to return to feed, bathe, and clothe the stranger. Odysseus shows a very un-Greek modesty at the thought of being bathed by the maids and asks that he be allowed to bathe himself. When he reappears, after having bathed and clothed himself, it is with a stature more majestic than usual. Nausikaa looks at him now with simple and undisguised admiration, confessing aside to her maids that when she is ready to be married, she hopes for just such a husband as this godlike stranger.

Comment

Nausikaa is portrayed as a very simple and reserved girl, but one who observes all good manners. Her desire is to marry someone strong and handsome like Odysseus, not necessarily Odysseus. The whole **episode** has dream-like qualities: a young girl is out on a bright summer's day, walks along the beach, and lets her mind wander; she feels ready for marriage and imagines a husband to fit the highest expectations; enter Odysseus. Whether the facts of the story are accurate or not is unimportant. They are all related from her point of view.

However willing she is to discuss marriage with the stranger, she is still observant of the Phaeacian proprieties. Odysseus must not be seen entering the town with her, for this would start unpleasant rumors. He should wait outside the city in her father's garden until he can enter the city without having people aware that she has seen and talked to him. Once in the palace he is to approach her mother and ask for her help in returning home.

Comment

It is not certain why Nausikaa has Odysseus ignore her father in his initial plea for help. An ancient commentator has suggested that the queen would be more likely to have pity on Odysseus; others have suggested Phaeacia might have been matriarchal.

The book ends as Nausikaa goes off to the city leaving Odysseus behind in a grove dedicated to Athena.

BOOK 7

Odysseus waits in Athena's grove until Nausikaa has had time to reach home; then he too sets out for the palace. Athena covers him with a thick mist so that he might pass unseen through the streets. But Odysseus himself is unaware of his invisibility, for when Athena approaches him in the guise of a young girl, he asks her for the way to the king's house. Athena warns him of the Phaeacians' mild hostility to strangers and suggests that he follow her without speaking to anyone. As he follows her, Odysseus notices the harbor and the well-built ships. (Nausikaa has already told him that the Phaeacians are not warriors, but shipbuilders and sailors) Athena gives him the same instructions as Nausikaa: to pass by the king (Alcinous) and supplicate the queen (Arete). As he enters the house, Odysseus marvels at the wealth of the palace.

Comment

The bronze walls, gold doors, and statuary suggest the splendor of the palaces that have been unearthed in Crete. It is therefore thought by some scholars that Homer was thinking of Crete when he described Scherie. Others (including the ancient Greek historian Thucydides) think Scherie sounds like Corfu.

The palace has fifty maids in constant attendance, most of them weavers. The women's skill in weaving equals that of the men in shipbuilding. Alcinous' garden is described: trees bear fruit the year round, grapes are always ready to be squeezed for wine, vegetables are constantly being produced by the fertile earth, and two springs ensure an unending supply of water.

Comment

The dream-like qualities of the encounter with Nausikaa continue as Odysseus enters the house of Nausikaa, which is incidentally her father's palace. The important element here is the fairy-land atmosphere which is suitable for young girls in love, but not for a Greek hero of Odysseus' temperament. Odysseus is a son of the island of Ithaca, where people scratch a living from the soil. The luxurious life of the Phaeacians surely grated, after a while, on his heroic nature. Greek heroes have never been able to survive on the rarefied air of luxury.

Odysseus enters the palace and, obeying Nausikaa's and Athena's instructions, clasps Arete's knees just as the mist about him is blown away. The king and queen are so startled at this strange visitor and his request that they remain silent, unable to answer. It remains for Echenaus, a Phaeacian nobleman, to remind the royal pair of their duty as hosts. Alcinous, thus prodded, offers Odysseus a place at his table and orders food and wine to be brought to him. Alcinous suggests to the assembled Phaeacians that they retire for the night and return in the morning when at greater leisure they can make plans for the stranger's return home. Alcinous compares Odysseus to a god, perhaps in the hope that Odysseus, when he denies that he is a god, will tell him his true identity. But Odysseus is too wily to be so tricked; he says that he is not built like a god and lets it go at that. He wants to eat before he talks.

Comment

Observe how quickly Odysseus gains command of the situation. He is able to manipulate the elders of the court as easily as he did the young Nausikaa, for the Phaeacians, unaccustomed to strife, are just like children when compared to the worldly Odysseus.

After dinner is over and the guests have left, Arete asks Odysseus who he is and where he comes from. She has noticed that he is wearing a garment that she herself had woven, and is curious as to how Odysseus obtained it. She also asks him about his journey to their land. Odysseus answers her last question first and then fits the story of Nausikaa's giving him the clothes into chronological order. It is not until the next book that he discloses his name and homeland. So charmed is Alcinous by his guest that he declares that nothing would please him more than to have Odysseus remain in his court as his son-in-law. But if this cannot be, he will have Odysseus taken to his home, no matter how far away. With his usual diplomacy, Odysseus mentions nothing in his reply to Alcinous of his suggestion that he marry Nausikaa; he does react favorably to the idea that he leave for home the next day (in point of fact, he leaves two days afterwards). Arete, like the good hostess she is, had, during the conversation, given orders that a bed be prepared for Odysseus. The book ends as all present go to bed.

BOOK 8

Early the next morning Alcinous calls an assembly. The Phaeacians, eager to see the mysterious stranger, crowd into the meeting hall. Alcinous proposes that Odysseus be conducted home.

Comment

Alcinous disturbs the whole routine of Phaeacian life just to call an assembly of two-minute duration. He does it to amaze the people and show off his guest, and to announce Odysseus' trip home. Alcinous is the king and needs no approval. The assembly is pure show. The people crowd into the place of assembly because they need something to do. If they were Greek heroes they would be bored with their land of milk and honey. In Homer's lifetime existence was not any easy matter, and such a place as this may have temporarily intrigued Homer as a splendid alternative to the hard life of Greece in 800 B.C. In his *Works and Days* Hesiod supports the anti-Phaeacian quality of life in Greece.

The court bard, Demodocus, who is blind, is summoned to entertain the guests. He chooses to sing a tale of the Trojan War: the story of the quarrel between Odysseus and Achilles.

Comment

There have been two conflicting reasons given for this quarrel: (1) Achilles was annoyed that he was not invited to a dinner; (2) Achilles and Odysseus were debating the means of overthrowing Troy. But the actual story of the quarrel does not matter as much as the fact that when Odysseus finally identifies himself, he will be known to the Phaeacians. Note also that Demodocus is blind, just as Homer was reported to be.

Odysseus starts weeping as he hears of his now dead comrades. By covering his head, he hides his sorrow from all but Alcinous, who is seated at his side. The king, without knowing the cause of Odysseus' grief, tactfully suggests that the games begin now. These games draw all the young nobles, some of whom are listed by Homer. All their names reflect involvement with the sea (e.g., "Nauteus" can be translated as "Seaman").

All the standard Greek sports are represented: running, wrestling, jumping, discus-throwing, and boxing. Laodamas, Alcinous' son, invites Odysseus to take part in the exercises. When Odysseus curtly refuses, Euryalus, a companion of Laodamas, insults him, saying that Odysseus is no athlete, but merely a merchant, interested only in making money.

Comment

This insult illustrates the typical Greek disregard for people who earn their living by buying and selling.

If Euryalus wanted to goad Odysseus into taking part in the athletics, he succeeded, for Odysseus, after delivering a speech twice as insulting as Euryalus', picks up a weight and throws farther than any other contestant. Now that he has been put to the test, Odysseus challenges all comers (except Laodamas, the son of his host) in all events.

Alcinous apologizes to Odysseus for the insult he has suffered. He also apologizes for the "weakness" of Phaeacian youth. It is true, he says, that we like games, but our greatest pleasure lies in dancing, music, and eating. So even if we are not the greatest athletes in the world, there is still plenty to praise us for.

Alcinous calls on Demodocus to dispel the awkwardness. The bard sings of the seduction of Aphrodite, Hephaestus' wife, by Ares, and tells how Hephaestus, the god of fire and crafts, when he learned of Aphrodite's unfaithfulness, devised a trap over their bed. The next time Ares and Aphrodite lay together in the bed, the nets fell on them and locked them in an embrace. Hephaestus called all the other gods to the bedside (the goddesses were too modest to come). After much laughter, Hephaestus released the pair, assured that Ares would pay him a fine for his misdeed.

Comment

Demodocus' song about the quickie-affair of Aphrodite and Ares is only one of many tales about errant deities. The only difference between gods and men was that man was mortal. The standard of ethical conduct of the supreme god, Zeus, was well below that of most mortals. He had affairs with Danae, Europa, and Alcmena-to name some. In the *Odyssey* Calypso, Circe, and Helen are hardly paragons of feminine virtues. All stand in stark contrast to Penelope, faithful forever.

After Demodocus' song, Alcinous asks his two sons, Halius and Laodamus, to give a demonstration of their dancing ability. They display their grace in a dance which is performed with a ball. Pleased that Odysseus liked the dance, Alcinous suggests that the nobles each give a gift to Odysseus. By nightfall Odysseus has received all his gifts, including a bronze sword from Euryalus, the lord who had insulted him earlier in the day. Queen Arete has the Phaeacians' gifts to Odysseus packed in a chest.

Nausikaa, who had been modestly standing by one of the pillars, comes forward to say hello to Odysseus. His reply (the last words he speaks to her before leaving) abounds in the guile he had used in speaking to her before; his role as Prince Charming in this fairy tale is over.

During the following meal, Odysseus honors Demodocus by offering him a cut of meat from the main table. Odysseus, forgetting for the moment how he reacted before to hearing of his comrades, asks Demodocus to sing the story of the Trojan horse. This the bard proceeds to do, taking the tale up at the place where the Greek forces had destroyed their camp in order to delude the Trojans into thinking that they had left for home. The horse was supposedly left as a monument to appease the gods. Some of the Trojans were suspicious of the horse, but they were overruled. They took the horse within their city's walls. Under cover of night they were overrun by the Greeks who were in the horse. Odysseus fought and won a mighty battle. Odysseus once more falls to weeping at these memories. And once again Alcinous notices this and asks that the music be stopped. Alcinous uses this opportunity to satisfy his (and everyone else's) curiosity and asks Odysseus who he is.

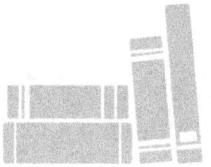

THE ODYSSEY

TEXTUAL ANALYSIS

BOOKS 9-13

BOOK 9

Comment

At this point Homer halts the action of the plot and provides us with a flashback to provide background material. The next four books (9-12) contain all of Odysseus' adventures from the end of the Trojan War until he reached Calypso's island, where we first met him in Bk. 5. The reader is reminded that Bks. 1-4 concerned the movements of Telemachus, and that we are not introduced to the hero until Book 5. Until we reach Bk. 13, almost all the *Odyssey* is scene-setting. Except for Odysseus' trip from Calypso's island to the land of the Phaeacians, the first half of the *Odyssey* (13 out of 24 books) acts as an introduction to the main plot, the return of Odysseus to Ithaca. But this introductory, part of the *Odyssey* is by all odds the most famous and best loved section.

Odysseus, called on to recount his adventures, proceeds, as any after-dinner speaker would, with a short introduction praising his host for the food and music. He names himself and his homeland, praising both, and then launches into the long story of his adventures. The first people Odysseus and his crew encountered were the Cicones, allies of the Trojans. Odysseus and his men sacked one of the Ciconian cities; but instead of leaving immediately with their booty of goods and slaves, the crew, against Odysseus wishes, stayed to feast on the Cicones' livestock.

Comment

Odysseus gave the order to plunder, not because he disliked these friends of his former enemies, but because he was greedy. Piracy was an accepted occupation among the seafaring Greeks, and Odysseus proved no exception.

The Cicones warned their inland neighbors of the attack. These were tougher folk than their seafaring neighbors and were able to drive the Greeks out, killing seventy-two of them. For twelve days Odysseus and his crew encountered alternate periods of storm and calm as they tried to sail home. They finally stopped at the land of the Lotus-eaters, a race of people, perhaps located in North Africa, who continually ate the lotus plant. This plant contained a drug that was a super-tranquilizer. Having eaten the plant, two of Odysseus' crew abandoned all thought of ever returning home to Ithaca. Odysseus dragged these two into the boat and had them put in irons; he then gave orders to set sail immediately so that no others of the crew might eat the lotus.

Comment

The land of the Lotus-eaters is a drug-culture Utopia. It is Homer's vision of a "brave new world" where the drugs are natural but could just as easily be called "soma." Odysseus' description of the land of the Lotus-eaters must have reminded the Phaeacians of themselves and their own land. One land is a double of the other; the land of the Lotus-eaters, however, is an extension and a heightening of the situation in Phaeacia. In Phaeacia all war and fighting had been eliminated, but there were still traces of strife present in their games. In the land of the Lotus-eaters, even these small remains of strife are absent. They are a people without any conflict at all, which is to say, they are not really human, for man depends on conflict, or at least interaction, to bring out and develop their humanity, e.g. Odysseus.

After they have escaped from the Lotus - eaters, they come to the land of the Cyclopes. These people are rustic, one-eyed barbarians who neither cultivate crops nor have any body of laws. They have no assemblies, not because they have no need of them, as is the case among the lethargic Lotus-eaters, but because they know that they would not obey any decisions reached by an assembly.

Fortunately, Odysseus and his men landed at night during a heavy fog, so that they were undetected by these fierce people. At dawn, the crew caught and killed some of the wild goats that climbed the rocky coast. The first day was spent in feasting on the goats and drinking the wine that they had stolen from the Cicones.

On the next day. Odysseus succumbed to his curiosity and went exploring with twelve of his comrades in order to see what sort of men inhabited this land. Odysseus took a goatskin containing fine wine. This was put to good use later. They made their way to a cave which was surrounded by pens of sheep and goats. Since the owner was away, they went inside the cave, where they found young lambs and goats and a lot of cheeses.

The crew were all anxious to leave after they had stolen the cheese and young animals. Odysseus, however, insisted that they stay to see the owner.

Comment

The trouble about to fall on Odysseus is his own fault. Usually his men cause the misfortunes. Odysseus is a curious man, interested in another peculiar man. He is more intrigued by the owner of the cave than by its contents. He is unafraid of the cave's owner. Heroes should know little fear; it is acceptable if little people (Odysseus's men) are afraid.

They made a fire over which they cooked one of the Cyclops' animals. At last the Cyclops returned, bringing his flocks with him. Before he sat down to milk the sheep and goats, he picked up a huge boulder to block the entrance to his cave. When he saw Odysseus and the crew, who had been huddling in a corner since the Cyclops' arrival, he demanded to know who they were.

Comment

This seems to us to be normal curiosity on the part of an owner of a house who discovers intruders. But it must be compared to the normal Greek practice, which we have seen so often before, of first asking a stranger to dine.

Odysseus introduced them only as Greeks who had fought in the Trojan War and wisely did not reveal his own name or the location of his ship. He asked the Cyclops for the rights due to travelers. In answer to this, the Cyclops, whose name was Polyphemus, grabbed two members of the crew and ate them.

Odysseus dared not kill Polyphemus because (at least, this is the reason he gives) they would be stuck in the cave, unable to move the boulder away from the entrance.

The next morning, Polyphemus ate two more men before taking his flocks to pasture, keeping the remaining Greeks locked in the cave. Odysseus frantically sought an escape plan and finally hit upon a scheme. He had his men cut and sharpen a wooden stick which Polyphemus had left. When Polyphemus returned that evening, Odysseus gave him the strong wine he had brought with him. While the Cyclops was tipsy from the wine, Odysseus told him that his name was Noman. At this point Polyphemus fell down in a deep sleep. Odysseus and his men quickly grabbed the sharpened stick, which they had heated in a fire, and rammed it into the Cyclops' one eye. They then scurried to the corners of the cave, so that the enraged and now blind Polyphemus could not grab them.

Roaring with pain, Polyphemus called for his fellow Cyclopes to help him. But, when they came and asked who was bothering him, he could only reply that "Noman" was killing him. His neighbors left in disgust. But Odysseus' troubles were not over-he still had to get out of the cave. Once again his cunning mind devised a plan. He and all his men tied themselves to the undersides of Polyphemus' sheep and were let out by Polyphemus himself.

Exulting in his cleverness, Odysseus could not resist shouting out his real name to Polyphemus, who was staggering about on the shore. Now that Polyphemus knew who his enemy was, he could pray to his father, Poseidon, asking him to give Odysseus as much trouble as possible. He then picked up a boulder and heaved it in the direction of Odysseus' taunting voice. The Greeks rowed away as fast as they could and rejoined the other ships which were waiting for them. After a day of feasting on the spoils from Polyphemus' cave, they set out for new adventures.

BOOK 10

The next land they reached was the floating island Aeolia. This was the home of Aeolus, the god who was given command over all the winds. Aeolus had six sons and six daughters whom he loved so much he had the sons marry their sisters so that they could all stay together.

Odysseus stayed with Aeolus as an honored guest for a month, exchanging gossip with him. At the end of this time, when it came time for Odysseus to leave, Aeolus presented him with a leather bag that held captive all the destructive winds. Summoning a favorable breeze, Aeolus saw them off on a trip which should have taken them directly to Ithaca.

After ten days of sailing, they were in sight of their native land. At this point, Odysseus made the error of falling asleep. The crew, who had been growing increasingly curious about the leather bag Odysseus always kept at his side, took this opportunity to see if they were being cheated out of some gifts. As soon as they undid the wire holding the bag closed, the winds rushed out with a blast of pent-up fury. Odysseus woke in time to find Ithaca fading rapidly out of sight as the ships were buffeted by the winds. The ships managed to stay together and were all blown back to Aeolus' island.

Odysseus went once more to Aeolus and asked him again to tie up the winds, so that they might attempt for a second time to reach Ithaca. Aeolus, however, took Odysseus' first failure as a sign that he was the enemy of the gods and that he should no longer be helped.

Downhearted, Odysseus returned to his waiting crew and told them the bad news. Now all the winds had left them and they were forced to row the long ships. After six weary days, they came to the land of the Laestrygonians. This land was so far north that the nights were extremely short.

All the ships but that of Odysseus sailed into a narrow harbor before dropping anchor; Odysseus wisely (as it turned out) anchored his ship outside the harbor. He then sent three of his men to investigate, for he had seen smoke rise over the hills.

These three men met the daughter of the Laestrygonian king, who directed them to her father's house. There they encountered the queen, a woman so large that they hated her on sight. She called her husband, who jumped on the men, for the Laestrygonians were cannibals. Two of the three escaped, but they were followed by thousands of the Laestrygonians, who stood at the edge of the cliff over-looking the ships and pelted the boats and men with huge boulders. They harpooned the dying men and took them home to eat.

Comment

Odysseus' crew and Penelope's suitors have a great deal in common. Homer occasionally reminds us of their similarities. Both groups illegally slaughter cattle and both are likened to fish, the crew here, the suitors in Book 22. Both animals, cattle and fish, are typically thought of as traveling in groups. Thus the comparisons we have been making between groups and between individuals enable us to make a higher comparison and one more important to the meaning of the *Odyssey*: a comparison between man as an individual and man as a member of the community.

Odysseus, whose ship was outside the harbor, saw that he could do nothing for his men trapped within. He sailed away on his one remaining ship and, after some time, reached the island of Aeaea. This was the home of the goddess Circe (Circe is Greek for "hawks"). After Odysseus had killed a stag and brought it back to his men, he reported that he saw smoke rising. His men, mindful of the Laestrygonians, pleaded with Odysseus to leave at once. But Odysseus would have none of this fright; it was against his nature to leave a land without knowing just what he was leaving. He split his men into two parties, assigning the command of the second party to Eurylochus. It was Eurylochus' group that discovered Circe's house. The goddess heard their shouts and invited them into her parlor. All but the suspicious Eurylochus entered. He remained outside, not knowing whether to trust Circe.

When Circe had what she thought was the whole group safely inside, she gave them a favorite Greek dish, a sticky mixture of cheese, grain, and wine. But there was something extra in this dish-a drug that turned them into swine. Eurylochus ran back to Odysseus to tell him of the misfortune that had befallen his party. Odysseus was determined to save them. He set off for her house and, on the way there, met Hermes, who gave him directions on how to deal with the beautiful goddess. He also gave Odysseus moly, a herb that had the power to counteract the drug Circe had given to his men.

Odysseus did as Hermes directed him, and soon Circe was in his power. She made Odysseus comfortable and granted his wish that she return his men to human form. She then invited Odysseus and all his men to stay with her for as long as they desired. Odysseus left his men feasting in the house and returned to the other half of his crew, who were waiting nervously for word of their leader's and comrades' fate. When Odysseus came and told them what had happened, they were all eager to return and share in the feasting - that is, all except the still suspicious Eurylochus, who said that this would be the end of all of them. But he too went when he saw that no one was listening to his warnings.

They were treated so well by Circe that they stayed for a year, feasting every day. By the end of this time, his men were once more eager to travel home. When Odysseus told Circe that they were leaving, he was told by the goddess that before he could reach Ithaca he would have to visit the house of Hades, the god of the underworld. The north wind would blow his ship, she said, to the entrance to the underworld. From there, he should descend into the land of ghosts and speak to the prophet Teiresias, who would tell him all he need know about getting home.

After he had received these instructions, Odysseus told his men to make ready. In the bustle of leaving, they were unaware that one of their number, Elpenor, had fallen from the roof of Circe's house and had been killed. It was not until the last moment before leaving that Odysseus told his men that they must make their way to the underworld before attempting to sail to Ithaca. They were heartbroken at the thought, but could do nothing to sway him.

BOOK 11

Odysseus and his crew weighed anchor and let the ship be directed by a wind that Circe called up for them. They sailed all day until they were brought to a place that Circe had described. Here Odysseus, following the goddess' instructions, dug a trench a cubit long by a cubit wide (a cubit is a measure derived from the length of a man's forearm and is equal to 18-22 inches). Around the trench Odysseus poured three libations, first honey and milk, then wine, and then water. Over this he sprinkled barley and prayed to the dead. He then poured the blood of freshly slain sheep into the trench.

Comment

The ritual of digging a trench and pouring libations around it is surely in the realm of sympathetic magic. Odysseus' actions imitate an ancient inhumation rite. By such a trench bodies descended into Hades, and by another such trench Odysseus called them back into the world. Burial in the Mycenaean world usually meant inhumation, but Homer tells us that at Troy the bodies of the Greek soldiers were cremated. That the Greeks were fighting on foreign soil and preferred not to bury their men except in Greek soil is a good explanation for cremation of Greeks at Troy. This cremation/inhumation question has bothered students of Homer lately and is far from being solved. Cremation seems to have come into the Greek world with the Dorians ca. 1000 B.C., before which time the Mycenaean practice of inhumation apparently prevailed. Therefore, when Homer speaks of Greeks cremating their dead, is he guilty of allowing **anachronisms** into his story, since cremation came to Greece in 1000 B.C., and the dramatic date of his story is 1184 B.C.?

Odysseus' trip to the underworld apparently in later days became a literary motif, a topos. For example, in *Aeneid* (Bk. 6), Aeneas goes to the underworld to get instructions on his future actions and Aristophanes has an underworld journey in his *The Frogs*.

It is possible that these "literary" journeys have some religious significance. In the Greek Eleusinian mysteries part of the ritual has to do with the capture and journey of Persephone into the underworld (which cause a draught above the earth).

Summoned by Odysseus' action, the souls of the dead came forth, eager to drink the blood he had spilled. The first soul to come was Elpenor, the member of the crew who had fallen from Circe's roof. He pleaded with Odysseus to return to Aeaea and to cremate his dead body, so that he might properly enter the ranks of the dead. This Odysseus promised to do.

The next ghost to come forth was that of his mother, Anticleia. But Odysseus, following Circe's directions, restrained her from drinking the blood (which gives the dead the power to speak). He must first consult Teiresias (Elpenor did not need the blood to speak, since he had not yet been cremated.).

Teiresias was the next to come, and, although he didn't need the blood to speak, he drank some anyway to strengthen himself. The prophet told Odysseus that he and his men would come to the island of Helios, the sun-god, where a herd of cattle grazed on the land. Teiresias warned Odysseus that under no circumstances were they to harm Helios' cattle if they wanted to escape unharmed.

Comment

Odysseus comes to this island in Bk. 12.

Teiresias now tells Odysseus of the suitors in his house who must be slain.

Comment

The reader of this **epic** is prepared already at this point for the numerous and, in a way, senseless murders of the suitors in Bk. 22. By informing Odysseus at this time that the suitors will try to take his wife and property, Homer heightens the suspense and the need for Odysseus to push himself toward Ithaca. Actually, at the time Odysseus visits the underworld, three years after the end of the Trojan War, the suitors have not yet started to woo Penelope. But this is a small inconsistency, for Teiresias, as a prophet, would know the future as well as the present.

After he has slain the suitors, Odysseus is to leave Ithaca once more with an oar over his shoulder. He is to travel, says Teiresias, until he is so far from the sea that nobody recognizes the oar for what it is. Then Odysseus should offer sacrifices to Poseidon and return home. A quiet death will then be assured him. Before he left, Teiresias told Odysseus that if he allowed any of the ghosts to drink the blood, then they would be able to speak. Odysseus immediately let his mother's ghost drink the blood. Since she died after her son had left for Troy, Odysseus was concerned about her, as well as the still living members of his household. Anticleia assured him that Penelope was still faithful to him and that Telemachus was happy in Ithaca. Laertes, however, was grieving for the return of his son, and it was this same grief which brought Anticleia to her death. Odysseus was so happy to be talking to his mother that he wanted to embrace her, but she slipped through his arms, unable to come into contact with him.

THE ODYSSEY

After his mother had left, a procession of famous Greek women came forth. The first was Tyro, Aeolus' grand-daughter, who gave birth to two sons by Poseidon. Tyro was followed by Antiope and Alcmene, the mother of Heracles. Next came Epicaste, who unknowingly married her son, Oedipus. When she had discovered what she had done, she took her life by hanging herself.

Comment

The story of Oedipus and his mother has been told by the Greek tragedian Sophocles in his play *Oedipus Rex*, and by the Roman tragedian Seneca in *Oedipus*. Sigmund Freud has made much of this myth in his works on psychoanalysis, and in the field of literature the reader is encouraged to read Ernest Jones' *Hamlet and Oedipus* (1949).

Epicaste was followed by Chloris, the mother of Nestor; Leda, the mother of Helen of Troy and of Clytemnestra, who murdered her husband, Agamemnon; Iphimedia; Phaedra; Procris; Ariadne; Maera; Clymene; and Eriphyle.

Odysseus now interrupts his tale. Arete, the Phaeacian queen, is the first to break the silence; she asks that more gifts be heaped upon their guest. Alcinous seconds the motion and suggests that Odysseus stay till the next day. Our hero never was the sort to refuse gifts and he agrees to remain one more day. He continues with his story.

After the parade of women, the ghost of Agamemnon approached him. Odysseus had not known that he was dead, and we once more hear the story of his murder, this time by the murdered person himself. Agamemnon counsels him not to trust anyone, and to sail secretly into his home port. The next ghost is that of Achilles, the hero of the *Iliad*, who lamented the fact that he was no longer alive. His statement has become famous; "I would rather be the serf of a poor man than king of the dead." Odysseus gave him news of his son, Neoptolemus, then said good-bye to him as he strode away.

All the ghosts came crowding about Odysseus, asking for news of friends and relatives - that is, all but Aias, who was still angry at Odysseus for having won Achilles' armor after he died. Odysseus begged that he be forgiven, but Aias turned silently away.

Comment

Aias' silence has been called a "silence more sublime than speech" by Longinus, a Greek critic.

Odysseus then saw Minos, the judge of the dead, dispensing his decisions; Orion, the hunter whose form became a constellation in the sky; Tityos, who was punished by having vultures constantly peck at his liver, which always grew back; Tantalus, the great-grandfather of Agamemnon, who was punished by having food and water placed barely out of his reach, so that he constantly starved within inches of food and drink (we get our word "tantalize" from him); Sisyphus, who was sentenced to the task of rolling a huge boulder to the top of a hill just as he reached the topic would roll back down; and Heracles, the mighty hunter.

Odysseus finally mastered his almost insatiable curiosity and left. He returned to his ship and gave the orders to cast off.

BOOK 12

The first stop after leaving the underworld was Aeaea, Circe's island. There Odysseus fulfilled his promise to Elpenor to cremate his body and plant an oar on the mound over his ashes.

They once more partook of Circe's hospitality, as Odysseus told her what had happened to him in the Hall of Hades. The goddess gave him further instructions for his journey home. The first danger he would encounter would be the Sirens. Those two women beckoned to all passersby, promising that they would impart to them the knowledge of all events. In order to prevent their seduction by the Sirens, the crew should plug their ears with beeswax. Odysseus may leave his ears unplugged but he must be tied to the mast.

After they had rowed past the Sirens, they would have a choice of dangers; they could go either through the Wandering Rocks, the rocks that destroy even passing birds; or they might sail through a narrow sea-pass that was as dangerous as the Wandering Rocks. On one side of the pass was the cave of the monster Scylla, who would stick her six long necks down to the water level and grab sailors off their boats (Homer probably had a giant squid in mind). On the other side of the pass was Charybdis, a strong whirlpool, which could easily suck an entire ship into its vortex. Circe suggested that Odysseus keep to Scylla's side and lose only six men rather than the whole ship. After they had passed through this danger, Circe continued, they would come to Thrinacie, the home of Helios, the god of the Sun. She repeated Teiresias' warning that they must not kill any of his cattle, if they wanted to reach Ithaca.

It was dawn when Odysseus set sail. He pretended to tell his men exactly what Circe had told him, but he actually told them as little as was necessary. He plugged their ears as they approached the Sirens and allowed himself to be tied to the mast. The Sirens started their song at the approach of the ship.

Comment

The sirens by their exquisitely lovely voices lure sailors to their deaths. Sailors also approach the Sirens too closely in their attempt to learn the future from these prophetesses. On the Rhine river in Germany at a sheer cliff of rock a few miles south of Koblenz is a place known as the Lorelei, made famous by the German poet Heine. Here a lonely maiden is, by tradition, to have sung to passing sailors and lured them to their deaths. Like the word "odyssey" which means trip, the word "siren" has come into the English language and means an alluring song or woman.

Thanks to Circe's warning, they passed safely by the Sirens. They soon came to the pass of Scylla and Charybdis, about which Circe had warned Odysseus. He gave orders to his crew to sail along one side as fast as they could, if they wanted to avoid disaster.

Comment

Odysseus cleverly avoided telling his crew that six of them were to be seized by Scylla.

Odysseus armed himself, but it did no good, for Scylla took her toll as they passed by. As they approached the island of the Sun, Odysseus gave his men the warnings he had received from Teiresias and Circe concerning the cattle of the Sun. He suggested that they pass by the island to avoid any possibility of danger.

The men, however, were exhausted from their ordeal with Scylla and Charybdis. Eurylochus, who, in Bk. 10, discovered Circe's magic, pleaded with Odysseus to allow them to rest overnight on the island. He promised that they would not harm any of the cattle. The crew applauded his speech so heartily that Odysseus acceded to his request.

Unfortunately, after they beached their ship, the South Wind started to blow and continued blowing for an entire month. At the end of this time, their supply of food ran out, and they were forced to try their hand at fishing and catching birds. Odysseus went inland to pray for aid. Eurylochus took advantage of his absence to suggest to the crew that they slaughter some of Helios' cattle. They could, he said, pay him back later in the form of a temple. The men agreed to this plan and proceeded to kill and roast some cows. Just then Odysseus returned. When Helios learned of what had happened, he complained to Zeus. He demanded that Zeus punish Odysseus-if not, he would go to the underworld and shine only among the dead. Faced with this threat, Zeus had no choice but to grant Helios' wish. (Odysseus interrupts his story to tell us that he knows of this from Calypso, who, in turn, heard if from Hermes.)

Odysseus raged when he saw his crew's sacrilege, but nothing could be done to correct the situation. Then, the cowhides began to crawl along the ground, and the cuts of meat began to moo. The men ate the meat nevertheless. On the seventh day after they slaughtered the cattle, they were able to sail from the island. This calm, however, was a trap, for as soon as Zeus had them in open water, he set a hurricane upon them that broke the boat and drowned all but Odysseus, who managed to make a crude raft from the wreckage of the boat and thereby stay afloat.

The storm blew him back to the pass of Scylla and Charybdis. Charybdis sucked down his raft, and would have sucked him down too, had he not grabbed hold of a fig tree which was growing on the face of the cliff. There he clung until Charybdis released his raft. He paddled away as quickly as he could to avoid meeting Scylla. After nine days of paddling, he came to Calypso's island, where we first met him in Bk. 5.

BOOK 13

Odysseus had just finished his long tale. The silence in the hall is broken by Alcinous who suggested that, in addition to the gifts they have already given him, the Phaeacians should present Odysseus with a tripod and a cauldron. They (the nobles) will be repaid afterwards by asking the people of Phaeacia to pay for the gifts given to Odysseus.

Comment

Here we see how seriously the business of "gifts" was taken. In a world without national states, travelers were dependent on the hospitality of the people with whom they stayed. Gifts were exchanged as a means of payment. These gifts were usually objects made of metal that were rarely used, but rather kept to be given away. Anyone who gave a gift expected a gift in return. When Athena refused Telemachus' gift in Bk. 1 because she was a goddess and could not accept a gift while in human form, she told him to hold off giving her a gift until her return. Then he should give her a worthy gift, she said, one that would bring him a worthy one in exchange. In other words, the gift-giving procedure was so well established that Alcinous was (in our terms) asking his people to pay a tax to finance a state function.

The next day Alcinous makes sure that the boat is in readiness to take Odysseus home. And Odysseus is very anxious to go home, constantly glancing at the sun until the time for departure. In his farewell speech, he thanks them for their gifts and prays the gods will bring no evil to them. (As we will soon see, the gods will indeed bring evil to them.) Odysseus now leaves the palace for his ship, accompanied by a servant of Alcinous and a group of Arete's maids. When they reach the boat, the young noblemen who will row him home take his gear, not allowing Odysseus to do any work for himself.

Comment

The Phaeacians do everything possible for the comfort of their guest, Odysseus. They are blameless hosts. Their action in taking Odysseus home is, in fact, more than was expected of hosts. In return for their kindnesses the Phaeacians are destroyed by vindictive gods. Morally and ethically the mortal men are better than their gods. Homer goes to some lengths to show the superiority of the mortals in this case. For Homer and the early Greeks their gods were neither just or merciful. Gods were gods because they were stronger than men and because they were immortal. Later philosophers argued about the nature of their gods and the meaning of justice as it comes from the gods.

The ship moves quickly and soon is beached in a calm inlet in Ithaca. Odysseus, who had fallen into a deep sleep during the journey and had not yet awakened, is lifted gently by the Phaeacians and placed by an olive tree. Next to him the

Phaeacians place their gifts. They leave without awakening Odysseus.

> **Comment**

This is the second time the olive tree has been mentioned in the *Odyssey*. The first time, at the end of Bk. 5. Odysseus had just dragged himself onto the Phaeacian shore. Beneath two olive trees he fell asleep. Here, too, the olive tree is associated with a deep sleep (Homer calls is "death-like"). The cave near the Ithacan olive tree is the equivalent of the protective covering of the Phaeacian olive tree. Both of them are womb-symbols which emphasize at strategic points in the poem the **theme** of rebirth.

Meanwhile, Poseidon, who sees that Odysseus has reached Ithaca, goes to Zeus to complain and asks that he be allowed to punish the Phaeacians for what they have done. Zeus suggests that Poseidon turn the Phaeacian ship into a rock just as it approaches Phaeacia and then that he surround the city with a ring of high mountains, which will forever cut the Phaeacians off from the sea, the source of their livelihood.

Poseidon does turn the ship to stone. Alcinous, who sees the transformation of his ship, reveals a prophecy that his father had given him: Since Poseidon disliked the Phaeacians' good will toward all strangers, he would someday wreck a Phaeacian ship and surround their city with mountains.

Alcinous suggests that they promise never to receive strangers again and that they sacrifice twelve bulls to Poseidon, so that he may take pity on them and not shut them off from the sea. We never learn how successful they are in their prayers, for just at this moment the scene switches back to Ithaca. Odysseus has just awakened and, after his long absence, does not recognize his native land. He thinks that the Phaeacians have let him off in some strange place. Then he counts his gifts to see if any have been taken.

Comment

In the twentieth year of his exile from Ithaca, Odysseus returns, and is amazed at not recognizing Ithaca when he awakens. We are reminded of prisoners of war who have returned home after many years in P.O.W. camps and the trouble they have in adjusting to radically changed conditions.

Odysseus asks a passing shepherd, who is really Athena in disguise, what land this is. She answers tantalizingly, holding back the name of Ithaca until the end of her speech. Odysseus, of course, is overjoyed to learn that he has finally reached his home. But Odysseus is too crafty to announce himself just yet and gives what is the first of his lying tales. Perhaps remembering the story of Agamemnon and his fatal homecoming, Odysseus decides to survey the situation before deciding on a plan of action. Athena is touched, amused, and proud of his long and elaborate lie (as a mother is who has just heard her child recite a poem). Athena is not above telling a few lies herself. So Odysseus, once he knows who she is, asks her if he is really in Ithaca, or was she lying to him, just as he lied to her.

After she assures him that he is home, the two of them plot their course of action. Athena helps disguise him, making him look like an old, bald beggar. Odysseus is to stay with his loyal swineherd, Eumaeus, while Athena summons Telemachus from Sparta.

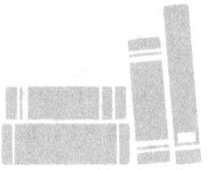

THE ODYSSEY

TEXTUAL ANALYSIS

BOOKS 14-18

BOOK 14

When Odysseus comes to the hut of Eumaeus the swineherd, he finds him sitting by the pigsty, shaping a piece of leather. Three of his assistants are out herding the pigs, while a fourth has gone to town with a hog for the suitors.

The dogs start barking as Odysseus, dressed like a beggar, approaches. They would have bitten him, had not Eumaeus driven them off with rocks. In his first words to this (supposed) stranger, Eumaeus bewails the fact that his king and master is away and perhaps not even living. But his grief doesn't stop him from fulfilling his duties as a host. He invites Odysseus into his hut, seats him on a modest but comfortable seat, and prepares some pork for him. If only Odysseus were here, he says, he wouldn't have to work any longer.

Comment

Notice how quickly Homer establishes Eumaeus' personality as a loyal, hard-working servant who doesn't hesitate to complain about his condition. He is one of the more memorable of the minor characters in the *Odyssey*.

As Eumaeus serves the food to Odysseus, he continues griping, this time about the suitors who keep pestering Penelope and who are eating up Odysseus' wealth. Odysseus asks him for his master's name. Perhaps, he says, he has met him in his travels. Eumaeus suspects that this beggar before him plans to go to Penelope with a lying story about Odysseus, so that he may be celebrated as the bearer of good news. Odysseus, pleased at this loyal outburst of indignation, promises Eumaeus that his master will soon be present once more in Ithaca. And as for Eumaeus' suspicion that he is prepared to lie, Odysseus is outraged. Why, he hates as much as the next fellow the man who is forced to lie because of his poverty (of course, he does lie-Odysseus thinks a person should lie out of a love for lying itself).

Eumaeus naturally does not believe the prophecy of the stranger and suggests that they talk about less painful topics. Now that the meal is over, custom permits that Eumaeus ask him his name and ancestry.

Odysseus, inventive as always, refuses, as a point of honor, to tell the same story to Eumaeus that he told to Athena. This time, he says that he was the son of a wealthy Cretan by a concubine. He develops an elaborate autobiography, including a rise from rags to riches, heroism on the battlefields of Troy, a seven-year stay in Egypt, a near miss at being sold as a slave, and a short stay in Thesprotia. It was there, he lies, that he heard of Odysseus. He says that the king told him that Odysseus has stopped there on his way home with a vast amount of wealth gotten from Troy and that from Thesprotia he went to the sacred oak tree in Dodona to seek advice on whether he should return home openly or in disguise.

Comment

This sacred oak tree was the most ancient source of the oracles of Zeus.

Odysseus continues his "tale." The king of Thesprotia offered him a ship to take him to Dulichium. The crew, however, stripped him of his fine garments with the intention of selling him into slavery. He escaped while they were off Ithaca and made his way to Eumaeus' hut.

Eumaeus is moved by this story, but refuses to believe the one bit of truth in it - that Odysseus is still alive. He remembers that once before a wanderer had told him that Odysseus was alive and would soon be back. Odysseus takes advantages of Eumaeus' skepticism to make an unfair bet with him. Eumaeus refuses to bet on what he thinks is a sure thing.

The assistant swineherds now enter the hut, complaining about the suitors. Eumaeus once more prepares some pork for his guest. As they eat, the evening air grows increasingly chilly. Odysseus, whose dress is too light for the cold, refuses to acknowledge this outright, and lets Eumaeus know it in as roundabout a way as possible. He says that, when, during the Trojan War, he, Odysseus, and some others went on a surprise raid, he didn't dress warmly enough for the occasion. While they were waiting for their chance to attack, he grew very cold. He told Odysseus of his condition. Odysseus suggested to the men that one of them run back to Agamemnon for reinforcements. When the "messenger" left his cloak behind so that he could run faster, he (the lying Odysseus) took it and so had protection against the frost.

Eumaeus is wise enough to realize that his guest is hinting that he would like some covering. He covers Odysseus with an extra blanket, but he himself does not lie down in the hut. He goes to spend the night among the swine to protect them from dogs and thieves.

Comment

Eumaeus does this out of a sense of duty to a master who he thinks is dead. This is a fitting ending to a book that has demonstrated so carefully and so well the loyalty of this humble servant.

BOOK 15

That same night Athena goes to Sparta to urge Telemachus, who had been staying all this time with Menelaus, to return home. Appearing to him in a dream, she puts various frightening thoughts into his head, some of them false, one of them true. Perhaps, she suggests, the suitors will take his property, maybe his mother will decide to marry one of them, and, who knows, maybe when she leaves the house to go with her new husband, she will take his property.

Also, Athena says, the suitors are waiting for him in ambush, so that, in order to arrive safely, he must sneak into Ithaca and stay at Eumaeus' hut until he can safely enter the town. Telemachus, aroused by this dream, wakes up Peisistratus, Nestor's son, and tells him that he is anxious to leave at once. Peisistratus wisely suggests that they wait until dawn; thus, they will have light to travel by, as well as gifts from Menelaus. And, indeed, Menelaus does assure him, after he learns of Telemachus' intention, that he will give him gifts. He has a meal quickly prepared while he goes to his store room to pick out gifts worthy of Telemachus. Helen, too, chooses gifts, garments that she herself has woven.

As soon as they finish their meal, Telemachus and Peisistratus prepare to leave. As Telemachus and Menelaus are saying their good-byes in the court, an eagle swoops down, holding a white goose from Menelaus' flock in its talons. Helen gives a favorable interpretation of this omen. Odysseus will return home and conquer the suitors as easily as the eagle has caught the goose.

Telemachus and Peisistratus leave Sparta and travel the whole day. They stay the night in Pherae, at the house of Diocles, and leave early the next morning, reaching Pylos before nightfall. Telemachus bids farewell to Peisistratus at his ship, thus avoiding a drawn-out interview with Nestor on shore. Just as his crew is ready to push off, a stranger runs up to them, asking to be taken on board. His name is Theoclymenus, and he belongs to one of the noblest of Greek families. He is able to trace his line back to Melampus, the first doctor and prophet, according to Greek myth.

Comment

Observe that although he is in danger of losing his life, Theoclymenus is so conscious of his own nobility that he demands to know Telemachus' pedigree before entering the ship.

THE ODYSSEY

Theoclymenus' story is similar to Odysseus' lying tales. Like them, and like the *Odyssey*, it is a story of an exile. He has killed a member of his own tribe and must escape the vengeance of that man's relatives and friends.

Comment

We are here given a very special insight into early Greek society. There were no written laws, nor, if there had been, was there any justice department to enforce such laws. Because there was no federal governmental structure throughout Greece or any police forces in the cities, crimes were avenged (not punished) by members of the family injured. Murder and any offences were matters to be settled between families, and were not a concern of the public at large. Mycenaean society was primitive; such societies, where families exist above or beyond any laws, have been the subject of close scrutiny by many anthropologists in this century.

Telemachus invites him to come along to Ithaca, where he will be made welcome. When all is in readiness, they set sail for Ithaca where the suitors wait in ambush. The scene changes abruptly to Eumaeus' hut, and it is not until later in this book that we learn of Telemachus' safe arrival in Ithaca.

At Eumaeus' hut, Odysseus is testing the swineherd's hospitality. He says he will go to town and, after telling his "tale" about Odysseus to Penelope, he will offer to be a servant for the suitors. In this way he will not be a burden to Eumaeus. Eumaeus tries to dissuade his guest from such a foolish act. First, he says, he runs the risk of being beaten by the suitors in one of their drunken rages; second, they prefer pretty, young boys as servants, not old beggars. Stay with us, Eumaeus pleads, you're welcome here. Telemachus will care for you.

Odysseus agrees and, to pass the time until Telemachus' arrival, he asks about his parents. Of course, he has learned of his mother's death and his father's seclusion from his mother's ghost (Bk. 11). We, the readers, however, learn something new - that Odysseus has a sister, perhaps more than one. Her name is Ctimene, and she lives with her husband in Samos.

Comment

According to some Greek writers, her husband was Eurylochus, the most outspoken member of Odysseus' crew. In the next book, we learn that Odysseus had no brothers.

Odysseus also asks the swineherd about himself. We now learn that this faithful swineherd is of noble blood (remember that, in Homer's time, a nobleman was anyone who owned his own house and land). While still a baby, he had been kidnaped from his parents by a maid who ran off with traders. When the maid fell overboard, the traders sold Eumaeus to Laertes, Odysseus' father.

As Odysseus and Eumaeus talk, Telemachus and his crew land in Ithaca. Telemachus plans to go straight to Eumaeus' hut, and not wanting Theoclymenus, his passenger, to drop in unannounced on Penelope, Telemachus directs him to the house of Eurymachus, one of the suitors.

While he is giving Theoclymenus directions, Telemachus is interrupted by an omen similar to that which occurred in Sparta at the beginning of this book: a hawk carrying a dove flies by, an act interpreted by Theoclymenus as an omen that Telemachus will have what he wants. Telemachus, pleased at this, now suggests that Theoclymenus stay with his friend and crew member Peiraeus.

BOOK 16

Odysseus and Eumaeus are eating breakfast when Telemachus arrives. Eumaeus, overjoyed at the sight of him, upsets his bowls in his haste to embrace and greet him. Telemachus expresses concern for his mother and is assured by Eumaeus that she is still faithful to her husband.

Odysseus, true to his role of beggar, rises to give his son a place at the table. Respecting the apparent age of this old beggar, Telemachus politely refuses to take his seat. From Eumaeus he hears Odysseus' lying tale of exile from Crete. Eumaeus suggests that Telemachus take him home.

Just as he was ashamed to entertain Theoclymenus in his house (end of Bk. 15), so now he admits that he is ashamed to bring this stranger home. His mother, he says, is distraught from the perpetual overtures of the suitors, and the suitors enjoy fighting too much to allow Telemachus to entertain guests. He offers instead to give Odysseus new clothes and passage to wherever he wants.

Comment

When we last saw Telemachus in Ithaca (Bk. 2), he made a stand against his mother's suitors, but we never learned whether or not he had some small success. He did not, and was in fact almost driven from his own house. His subsequent search for information about his father and his travels to Pylos and Sparta were surely motivated in part by fear of the suitors and his desire to avoid another humiliating confrontation.

Odysseus tries to spur his son into action against the suitors. If he were Odysseus' son, he says, he would not put up with the suitors' shenanigans. He would beat them single-handedly if he had to. The only answer Telemachus can make to this is that since he has no brothers to help him, he could never prevail. He sends Eumaeus to tell his mother that he is back in Ithaca. The swineherd reminds him how unhappy his grandfather, Laertes, is-he mopes about his farm all day, hardly eating. Eumaeus wonders if he shouldn't stop off and tell Laertes too that Telemachus has returned. There is no time for that, says Telemachus, just tell Penelope.

After he leaves, Athena appears to Odysseus and calls him outside, advising him to reveal his identity to his son, so that the two of them may plan together to rid the palace of the suitors. Odysseus, without his disguise, re-enters the hut, stunning Telemachus with his appearance. His son can hardly believe his eyes and declares that this person before him is a god. Odysseus manages to convince him that he is his father, and the two fall to weeping. After this, Odysseus learns from his son that there are 108 suitors in his house, a number too large, says Telemachus, for the two of them to take on by themselves.

But, says Odysseus, we have Zeus and Athena on our side, and that makes all the difference. But Odysseus is not so foolish as to depend entirely on the gods' help without a clever plan of his own: Telemachus and he (once more disguised as a beggar) are to go to the hall where the suitors eat. At a nod from Odysseus,

Telemachus is to gather all the weapons that are lying about the hall, leaving weapons only for the two of them.

Before they do this, Telemachus must promise not to tell anyone that Odysseus is back, not Eumaeus, not even Penelope. They must also find out who among the servants is still faithful. By now Telemachus is convinced that they don't need any help from the servants and that they are only wasting time making plans.

Comment

Although Telemachus protests that he is not immature, in actuality he shows that he is not yet grown up. When he thought that his father wanted only the two of them to slay the suitors (something he should have known his father was too clever to attempt), he rejected the idea. When he learned that his father had a plan which included the aid of other people, he suddenly became anxious to fight immediately and without help.

Meanwhile, a messenger from Telemachus' ship has announced publicly that Telemachus has returned. The suitors are angry that he has escaped their ambush. As they plan to send news to the ship waiting in ambush, they spot it sailing into the harbor. Once all the suitors are assembled, Antinous suggests that, if they are to settle the matter of their courtship successfully, either they must slay Telemachus and divide the property among themselves, or they must each go to his own home and court Penelope in the accepted manner. If they don't do either of these, Telemachus will call another assembly and denounce them for their attempted ambush. Amphinomus, another suitor, suggests that they put the matter before the gods.

Penelope now appears before the suitors. She has heard of the attempted ambush and has come down from her room to denounce the suitors, Antinous in particular, for being cowards and double-dealers. Eurymachus takes it upon himself to answer Penelope's charges. He denies that he ever had, or ever will have, a part in any attempt on her son's life. Penelope returns to her room, where she cries herself to sleep.

When Eumaeus returns to his hut, he tells Telemachus and the re-disguised Odysseus of the ship of armed suitors he saw returning. The book ends, as so many of the books do, with everyone going to sleep.

BOOK 17

At dawn, Telemachus announces that he is returning to the palace to see his mother. He asks Eumaeus to take Odysseus to the palace later in the day, so that he may try his hand at begging scraps from the suitors' table.

The first person Telemachus sees on entering his house is the nurse Eurycleia. They greet each other with tears-until Penelope, leaving her room, sees her son. Telemachus cuts her short when she too starts weeping. He must, he says, go to the marketplace to fetch Theoclymenus, who has spent the night with his friend Peiraeus.

Once in the marketplace, he is surrounded by the suitors, who pretend great concern for his health, all the while thinking how they might best kill him. Theoclymenus comes with Peiraeus, then accompanies Telemachus back to the palace, where they bathe and eat. Penelope, who is present during their meal, can no longer contain her curiosity-what has Telemachus learned about the whereabouts of Odysseus, she asks.

Telemachus briefs her on his trip to Nestor's Pylos and Menelaus' Sparta - and tells of their love of, and concern for, Odysseus; but only Menelaus had heard anything about him - that he was being held by Calypso in Ogygia, from which escape is impossible. Of course, Telemachus, obeying his father's orders, tells her nothing of what she would like most to hear: that Odysseus has not only left Ogygia, but is present in Ithaca. Theoclymenus, however, is not under orders, so he tells Penelope that, according to all the signs, Odysseus is in Ithaca plotting doom for the suitors. Penelope hopes that what he says is true.

Toward dinner time, Eumaeus offers to escort Odysseus into town before the evening grows chilly. Odysseus accepts the offer (of course he does; Eumaeus is acting under orders from Telemachus, who in turn is acting under orders from Odysseus) and in keeping with his role as a beggar, asks for a cane to lean on.

On their way to town, they meet Melanthius, a goatherd who is bringing two of his flock to the suitors for slaughter. Unlike Eumaeus, who has remained faithful to his absent master, Melanthius is willing and anxious to please the suitors, so that he may get on their good side. When he sees Eumaeus, whom he hates for being loyal, and his beggar-companion, he launches into a tirade, warning Odysseus that he will very likely get a beating, not food, from the suitors. As he passes them, he gives Odysseus a kick that nearly knocks him off the road.

This sets Odysseus fuming, but just as he is about to abandon his role as an old man and kill Melanthius, Eumaeus speaks up. He chides Melanthius for his bad behavior and accuses him of neglecting his work. Melanthius, of course, cares nothing for what Eumaeus thinks of him and continues on his way to the suitors.

Eumaeus and Odysseus arrive at the palace a few minutes after Melanthius, who by this time is dining with the suitors whom he loves so much to serve. In the palace courtyard, Odysseus notices his dog Argus ("Flash" would be the best modern equivalent of his name). This old dog recognizes his master, but is too weak to approach him; he can only wag his tail and droop his ears. Odysseus is quite moved at the sight, for he remembers how Argus and he used to hunt together, and it saddens him to see how decrepit this once proud hound has become. Argus, after waiting nineteen years to see his master again, now succumbs to his old age and quietly dies.

Once inside, Odysseus starts begging food from the suitors. He gets some scraps until that busybody Melanthius speaks up to tell everyone that Eumaeus brought him into town. This annoys Antinous, who insults Eumaeus for bringing this beggar to them. Eumaeus defends his right to bring guests to Odysseus' home and is backed up in this by Telemachus. Antinous becomes very angry and picks up his footstool to threaten Odysseus. Odysseus, now in the third of his lying tales, explains that he was once a nobleman himself and that he never refused a beggar anything. He accuses Antinous of being stingy. This insult from a beggar is too much for Antinous' pride. He hurls his footstool at Odysseus and hits him square in the shoulder. Odysseus stands up to the blow, then addresses the suitors.

Comment

The scene of the reception of Odysseus in his own house contains some of Homer's best **irony**. Odysseus is rejected in his own house by people who do not belong there. Their sense of power and well-being in being able to insult Odysseus only makes their final end so much more ironical. In Bks. 18 and 20 objects are also thrown at Odysseus. The scene where Odysseus meets his dog after twenty years and the dog's relief at now being able to die is a truly touching scene. The dog is in a way a counterpart to the faithful servant, Eumaeus.

Odysseus says that he hopes Antinous will never live to reach his wedding day.

Comment

The statement is ironical, for not only is it Odysseus himself who makes sure that Antinous never lives to reach his wedding day, but it is this "wedding day," i.e., Antinous' hoped-for wedding with Penelope, that is the cause of his death. That is, if he had never planned on marrying her, he would not have been killed.

When Penelope hears of this attack on a guest in her house, she summons Telemachus to ask him to invite the stranger to come before her. As she finishes speaking, Telemachus sneezes very loudly. Penelope interprets this to mean that her prayer will be answered - that Odysseus will return to kill the suitors.

Comment

Any action that was not "normal" was believed to be caused by a god. Sneezes fell into this category because they could not be controlled. They usually were considered good omens, so that, by the third century B.C., a Greek poet, Theocritus, could write,

"The goddesses of Love sneezed on Simichidas" implying that the goddesses favored him.

Eumaeus repeats to Odysseus Penelope's request for his presence. Odysseus asks the swineherd to tell Penelope that he will visit her that evening, thereby allaying any suspicions the suitors might have. Penelope agrees to this and waits for Odysseus.

BOOK 18

While Odysseus is waiting for the suitors' departure, so that he can visit Penelope unseen, a beggar enters the palace in search of food.

Comment

Though his name is Arnaeus, everyone calls him by the nickname Irus, which, like the name of the goddess Iris, the messenger of the gods, means "talker" or "speaker." He evidently received this nickname because, in his desire to please people, he would carry messages for them.

Either Irus knows that the suitors are not friendly to Odysseus or, what is more likely, he is annoyed at seeing another beggar in the hall receiving food that he feels is his. In any case, he immediately starts insulting Odysseus and orders him to leave. Odysseus says that Irus will have to throw him out if he wants to be rid of him. Irus, seeing an easy victory and extra food from the suitors for bruising Odysseus, accepts the challenge. The suitors, pleased at the thought of a fight, quickly crowd around the two beggars. As Odysseus adjust his rags so that they don't interfere with his fighting, the suitors catch sight of his muscular thighs and are amazed. Irus too has seen his legs-a sight that makes him sorry that he had started the fight. The suitors see his fear but are too bloodthirsty to allow him to back out. Antinous even threatens to give him to an evil giant if he does not go through with the fight. Irus, now quaking, faces Odysseus and is laid low with one smashing blow to the neck. Odysseus drags him out by his feet and props him against the courtyard wall like a scarecrow. Odysseus is congratulated by the suitors and offered bread by Amphinomus.

Comment

It was Amphinomus, you will recall, who, in Bk. 16, spoke to the other suitors against plotting Telemachus' death.

Odysseus tries, while concealing his identity, to warn Amphinomus of the impending slaughter. He says that if Odysseus ever comes back all the suitors' blood will be spilled. Amphinomus feels in his heart that what the beggar says is true, yet he does nothing to prevent it.

The thought now comes to Penelope to leave her room to speak to Telemachus even though this entails appearing before the suitors-something she prefers not to do. After a brief nap, during which Athena enhances her beauty with divine cosmetics, Penelope enters the hall where the suitors are congregated. Her appearance of course causes quite a stir among the suitors, but she goes straight up to her son and addresses him, chiding him for allowing his guest to be mistreated. Telemachus admits that he was wrong in allowing the fight to occur and feebly defends himself with the argument that Odysseus won the fight.

Comment

Once his father is back in the house Telemachus seems to relax and recover his manners. Because of the presence of the suitors in the house, the relationship between Telemachus and his mother was strained. Telemachus surely felt that his mother was waiting for him to drive her suitors out, and that consciously or unconsciously she was comparing him to his father. It is the old father-son rivalry, and in this case the son is found wanting.

Eurymachus breaks in, praising Penelope's great beauty. In response, Penelope bewails the fact that, now that it appears she must remarry, her choice is limited to such rude, cheap youngsters. The insult that they are cheap stings them most. They immediately sent for gifts of clothes and jewelry to impress her with their generosity. When darkness comes, the maids scurry about the palace, lighting torches for the suitors. This infuriates Odysseus, who knows that they should be helping Penelope. But when he offers to relieve them of their task, one of them, Melantho, the sister of the evil goatherd Melanthius, laughs at Odysseus' offer. She, like the rest of them, much prefers serving the suitors to helping her mistress. Odysseus' threat to tell Telemachus finally chases the maids back to Penelope. This makes the suitors angry at him once more. Eurymachus tries to provoke him by making fun of Odysseus' head, which Athena has made appear so bald that it reflects the torch light. After this insult, Eurymachus offers him a job as a serf.

Comment

The serf was the lowest person in the social hierarchy of free men. When, in Bk. 11, Achilles says that he would rather be a serf on Earth than king of the underworld, he means that the worst position on Earth is better than death. Obviously, Eurymachus is doing Odysseus no favor when he offers him this position.

Odysseus replies that if it ever came to a contest between the two of them in performing a serf's functions he (Odysseus) would win easily. Eurymachus, angered by this reply, follows Antinous' example and throws his foot-stool at Odysseus; but, unlike Antinous, he misses him, striking the servant pouring wine instead. This cowardly action so angers Telemachus that he orders the suitors from his house. Amphinomus accepts his rebuke and agrees to go, as eventually do the other suitors.

THE ODYSSEY

TEXTUAL ANALYSIS

BOOKS 19-24

BOOK 19

Odysseus is now ready to carry out the next phase of his plan - the clearing of arms from the hall. He reminds Telemachus of the plan and of the excuses he is to have ready, should the suitors notice what he is doing: that the arms are smudged from smoke and that a suitor might kill someone with one of the swords the next time he becomes drunk. Telemachus tells Eurycleia, the nurse, what he is doing, giving the damage done to the weapons from the smoke as his excuse. It pleases her that her young master is finally expressing an interest in the affairs of the house. As father and son carry the weapons through the house, Athena leads the way, holding a lamp that casts a mysterious gleam over the walls. Telemachus now goes to bed at his father's bidding. Odysseus, however, returns to the hall to keep an eye on his property and servants.

Penelope comes once more from her room to warm herself by the fire. Melantho, who has accompanied her mistress, again starts insulting Odysseus for being a tramp. In an angry speech, Odysseus reminds her that there is more than one kind of tramp. Penelope too is angry at Melantho for her insulting speech and invites Odysseus to sit at her feet. She asks him to tell her about his past. This request is politely refused by Odysseus, who claims that he becomes too sad whenever he recounts his history. Penelope, however, has no compunctions about telling her own story, especially that part of it which displays her cleverness. She tells at length about her unraveling of the shroud.

Now that she has told her story, she once more requests her guest to speak of himself. Nobody refuses a queen twice, not even her husband, and so Odysseus launches into the fifth of his lying tales. In this tale, he is again a Cretan, but not, as in the other stories, an exile. Once, he says, he entertained Odysseus in his home when a strong wind kept him in Crete for nearly two weeks. This first-hand report of her husband brings tears to Penelope's eyes, but her tears do not bind her to the possibility that this stranger is playing on her sympathies.

What did he look like? What did he wear? she asks, and who were his companions? Odysseus wisely answers only the last two questions, not wanting to bring it to Penelope's mind that her guest resembles her husband in many ways. His description of the clothes that Odysseus had worn and of his companions is enough to convince Penelope that he does indeed have first-hand knowledge of Odysseus. But now her guest has further news of her husband, news he received from the king of Thesprotia. It seems, he says, that Odysseus has had a great deal of trouble and has lost all his crew because his men killed the cattle of the Sun god. Now he is wandering about, amassing great wealth before he returns to Ithaca. He repeats the story that Odysseus had gone to the sacred oak in Dodona to learn how best to re-enter Ithaca-openly or in disguise. He promises her that Odysseus will be home before the end of the year.

Penelope rejects the idea that Odysseus will return. She now offers to have Odysseus washed by her servants before he goes to bed. Odysseus, remembering the harsh manner in which the younger maids have treated him, asks for an older servant to tend to his needs. Penelope honors his wish and asks Eurycleia to wash his feet. Eurycleia agrees to do this and notes how much he looks like her master. This reminds Odysseus of a scar on his leg which he has had since boyhood, a scar that the old nurse would be certain to recognize. She does indeed recognize the scar.

Comment

Just at the point where we expect some kind of reaction from Eurycleia, as she recognizes Odysseus from his scar, Homer breaks off the story for a long digression and history of the circumstances leading up to his acquiring that scar. The famous critic, Erich Auerbach, was so taken up by this digression that he devoted a whole chapter to it in his influential book, *Mimesis*, called "Odysseus' Scar". Auerbach believes that this **episode** of Odysseus' scar is a good example of Homeric art. Odysseus, Penelope and the nurse Eurycleia are all in the same room, when the nurse recognizes Odysseus' scar. Homer stops the action and describes in great and graphic detail how Odysseus grabbed his nurse with one hand and what he did with the other hand. Everything is told in a leisurely fashion without passion or a sense of urgency. Every little detail is covered including the description of gestures, and it is done in an orderly and illuminating way so that the audience or reader can understand every facet totally. Homer omits nothing. He outlines and illuminates his characters and their actions with the result that they "stand out in a realm where everything is visible; and not less clear - wholly expressed, orderly even in their ardor - are the feelings and thoughts of the persons involved." Auerbach calls this "externalization," the first process in a long road toward absolute **realism** in literature.

The story Homer tells is briefly this: Odysseus received the wound on a boar hunt during a visit to his grandfather, Autolycus. It was Autolycus who named him, giving him the name Odysseus from the Greek word odyssomai, meaning "to cause pain to someone" (the English word "anodyne," a pain-reliever, comes from the same stem). Many years after his birth Odysseus paid a visit to Autolycus. After spending the first day feasting, they planned a boar hunt for the second day. Odysseus and his uncles tracked a boar to its lair. This boar, hearing the approach of the hunters, sprang forth and gored Odysseus' thigh, just at the moment that Odysseus drove his spear through the brute's body.

Comment

Here is a moment that expresses the very nature of Odysseus' existence: he is living out both the active and the passive aspects of the meaning of his name - that is, he is both giving and receiving pain. Throughout the poem, Odysseus either brings pain to others or receives pain. Even to those he loves, he brings pain: to Anticleia, his mother, who died grieving over his long absence; to Penelope, who cries herself to sleep each night; and even to Argus, his dog, who dies upon seeing his beloved master return.

We now return to Eurycleia, who has just recognized Odysseus. She turns toward Penelope, whose attention is focused elsewhere, but Odysseus silences the old maid before she reveals his identity. She promises to keep his secret, then finishes washing his feet. When Eurycleia is gone, Penelope asks Odysseus for advice: should she still refuse the advances of the suitors, or should she marry one of them? She describes a dream in which an eagle slew her geese, then flew near, and began to interpret the dream for her. The eagle claimed that he represented Odysseus, who would slay the suitors.

Odysseus assures her that the dream's self-analysis is true, but Penelope is unconvinced. She reminds him of the myth of the two gates through which all dreams come - the ivory gate for false dreams and the gate of horn for true dreams. She is sure that this dream has come from the gate of ivory.

She is prompted to let a contest decide who shall be her husband.

The next day, she says, she will test the suitors' skill in archery. Odysseus encourages her in this enterprise and promises her that her husband will be there. They now part to go to sleep.

BOOK 20

As Odysseus prepares his bed, a party of maids passes by. The sight of these girls who have become the mistresses of the suitors infuriates him. Only the thought that he has had to suffer greater torments allows him to wait until he kills the suitors before he kills the maids.

But this raises the question of what his plan of killing the suitors will be. As yet, he has formed no definite course of action. Athena, appearing to him in the form of a young girl, assures him that he should have faith in her. She will always be by his side. Comforted by Athena's promise, he is able to fall asleep.

At the moment that Odysseus falls asleep, Penelope awakens in tears. She prays to Artemis, the goddess of the hunt, asking to be slain. She recalls the myth of the daughters of Pandareus, who were kept alive by Athena for many years, only to be seized on their wedding day by the winds. The cause of her grief, she says, is that she has just now had a most vivid dream in which Odysseus appeared.

At dawn, Odysseus awakens, imagining that Penelope is beside him, aware of his true identity. He goes outside to ask Zeus for a sign that he will succeed in his goal. He asks for a sign of a double nature: ominous words spoken by someone in the house coupled with an omen that will appear outside. Zeus obliges him, for as soon as Odysseus is done with his prayer, a thunderclap is heard. Then Odysseus hears one of his servants, who has been grinding wheat for bread, exclaim that this thunder, coming as it does from a cloudless sky, must be meant as an omen for someone. She, the servant, ends with a prayer to Zeus that this day will be the last she will have to grind grain for the suitors.

Comment

This day is the last day for the suitors and is also the most completely described day in the *Odyssey*, filling out Bks. 20, 21, and 22.

By now, Telemachus has arisen, and his first concern is for his father. He asks Eurycleia whether the beggar was properly attended (remember that Telemachus does not yet know that

Eurycleia is aware of the beggar's true identity). She assures him that he was well taken care of, then proceeds with her duties about the house, ordering the younger maids to sponge the tables and wash the cups.

Eumaeus now comes with three pigs (normally only one pig was consumed in a day, but today a feast is planned at which Penelope will announce her choice of a husband). While Eumaeus and Odysseus exchange greetings, Melanthius, the evil goatherd, approaches and once more insults Odysseus; Odysseus is brimming over with anger at this faithless servant, but says nothing. Another herdsman, Philoetius, arrives leading livestock. He expresses a friendly interest in Odysseus and welcomes him to Ithaca. Philoetius, who, like Eumaeus, loves to talk about the old times, reminisces about the good old days when Odysseus was master. Odysseus recognizes that he has a faithful servant in Philoetius, one who can be trusted to do his share in the fighting.

The scene now shifts to the main hall, where the suitors are once more thinking of how they might best kill Telemachus. Their discussion is interrupted by an eagle which soars down on their left, holding a dove in its claws. Amphinomus, who once before stopped the suitors from going ahead with their plan to kill Telemachus (Bk. 16), interprets the eagle's flight as a sign that they will not succeed in their plan.

By now, the hall is filled with diners and servants. Telemachus requests the suitors to **refrain** from drunken brawls. Antinous grows angry at the suggestion that the suitors need to be warned to keep the peace, but, as we see immediately, they do need such a warning. Ctesippus, a sarcastic suitor, offers Odysseus a "gift," a cow's hoof, which he tosses at Odysseus' head. Odysseus merely ducks and gives Ctesippus a nasty smile (knowing full well that he will soon have the pleasure of killing him). But Telemachus cannot control his anger so easily. He denounces the suitors and demands once again that they stop their brawls. Agelaus, one of the suitors, apologizes, then suggests what the suitors have been suggesting for years - that Penelope marry one of them. Telemachus replies that he has no desire to put off his mother's wedding, but were it up to him he would drive the lot of them from the house.

The suitors' reaction to what seems to be the granting of their request is strange: they start laughing; then they lose control so completely that they become hysterical and think that they see blood over all their food. Theoclymenus sees this scene for what it is-a **foreshadowing** of the doom to come. The suitors refuse to believe him and order him to leave, something Theoclymenus is all too happy to do before the slaughter starts. After this eerie scene, the suitors try to force things back to normal by again turning to Odysseus with insults.

BOOK 21

Penelope, carrying out the plan she outlined to Odysseus in Bk. 19, goes to the storeroom to find Odysseus' bow. Homer tells us the origin of this bow, which is to play an important role in the poem. It was given to Odysseus by Iphitus of Messene, whom Odysseus first met when he was a boy. Iphitus, in turn, received the bow from his father.

Penelope quickly locates the bow among the other objects stored away in the room. She cries as she touches it, so much does it remind her of her husband. But since she is determined to go through with her plan, she goes to the main hall and announces the contest to the suitors. Whoever, she says, displays the most skill in stringing the bow and shooting an arrow through the holes in twelve axe blades shall have the privilege of marrying her. She gives the bow to Eumaeus to hand over to the suitors, but the noble swineherd can only cry at the thought that Penelope has finally agreed to remarry. Philoetius too starts crying. Antinous mocks the two for their blubbering.

Telemachus, on the other hand, is so happy at the prospect of the contest that he breaks into laughter. He prepares the hall for the contest. Digging a trench in the dirt floor, he places the handles of twelve axes in a straight line so that the holes through which the axeheads are fastened are aligned. The aim of the contest is to shoot an arrow through all twelve holes. But before anyone can shoot, he must first string the bow-a formidable task in itself. Telemachus tries three times to string it. He would have succeeded on the fourth try had not Odysseus signaled him with a nod of his head to stop. Telemachus sees the nod and pretends to have failed; he then offers the bow, as yet unstrung, to the suitors.

The first to try is Leodes, but this effeminate young lad merely hurts his hands in the attempt. He finally admits that he will never be able to do it, and prophesies that the bow will bring trouble to many of the suitors present. Antinous, ever quick to take offense, makes fun of Leodes for prophesying doom merely because of his own weakness. Antinous turns to Melanthius and asks him to melt some animal fat so that they can grease the bow and thereby ease the task.

Meanwhile, Odysseus has noticed that Eumaeus and Philoetius have left the hall. He quickly follows and overtakes them in the courtyard, where he can speak to them secretly. He poses a "hypothetical" question: whose side would they be on if Odysseus suddenly were to return and do battle with the suitors? The herdsmen of course answered that they would fight, and fight hard, on the side of Odysseus. Odysseus, who does not need this final assurance, now reveals his identity to them, giving as proof the scar on his leg. He reveals his plan and asks their help; Eumaeus is to give the bow to Odysseus when he asks for it, and he is to tell the maidservants to stay in their rooms, no matter what noises they hear; Philoetius is to close the door to the courtyard so that no one may escape. Odysseus re-enters the hall, followed soon afterwards by the two herdsmen. The bow, which had been passed around during Odysseus' absence, now comes to Eurymachus.

Comment

Though Odysseus has been gone from Ithaca for twenty years, when he returns he naturally reassumes his regal bearing and confidence. He leaves the hall because he knows no one can string the bow and shoot it, and also to set up his plans with his two servants. Odysseus has that royal confidence seen in certain personages like great kings and queens who need not look behind themselves to see if the chair has been set in place by the servant. They have supreme confidence that it is. Odysseus' brief exit from the hall breaks the steadily rising tension among the characters and offers the reader a brief respite in the drama just prior to the denouement.

Eurymachus, too, fails in the attempt to string the bow. Antinous suggests that they put the remainder of the contest off until the next day-a plan that all the suitors agree to. Before they leave, however, Odysseus asks if he can have a chance at the bow. Antinous accuses him of being drunk and reminds him of the story of Eurytion the Centaur, who got drunk at a wedding party and ran wild until he was thrown out. Penelope wants the beggar to try his luck at the bow, though she is careful to add that even if he does string it, he must not expect her to marry him. Eurymachus replies that he is afraid that their reputations will suffer if an old beggar succeeds where they have failed. But Penelope insists that the beggar be given the bow. Telemachus wisely sends his mother out of the room before the blood starts to flow. Eumaeus carries the bow to Odysseus and then tells Eurycleia to keep the maidservants in their rooms. Philoetius, carrying out his orders, locks the courtyard door.

Odysseus examines the bow, ignoring the taunts of the suitors who make fun of the expert way he handles it. He strings the bow without the slightest difficulty and then plucks the string so that a note is heard throughout the hall. The suitors are struck dumb. A clap of thunder is heard. Odysseus picks up an arrow and, without seeming to aim, shoots it through all twelve axe blades. Telemachus moves to his side and the fight is about to begin.

BOOK 22

Odysseus tears off his beggar's clothes and leaps to the doorsill of the main entrance of the hall. He is exultant as he shouts, "This contest is over now - but there's another target I'd like to hit." So saying, he shoots an arrow that pierces Antinous' neck just as the suitor reaches for a cup of wine. The other suitors still do not know that the beggar is Odysseus, and they think Antinous has been slain by accident. They all spring from their chairs, threatening to kill this careless archer. Odysseus checks their advance: "You dogs didn't think I'd ever return home. Your death is fixed."

At these words, the color drains from their faces. The ever suave Eurymachus tries to save them by putting all the blame on Antinous. Antinous was a foreigner, pleads Eurymachus, but we are fellow Ithacans. You wouldn't kill us. But if you do plan such a deed, he continues, then accept a bribe instead and spare us. Odysseus tells them that no bribe will keep him from killing them. Eurymachus now addresses the suitors, telling them that their only salvation lies in rushing Odysseus in the hope that one of them will be able to escape and bring reinforcements.

Comment

The suitors are not completely unarmed (they still have their personal swords), but there are no extra spears. The ritual slaying of the suitors has many earmarks of a religious sacrifice. The gods in the person of Teiresias in Hades had ordered it done, and Odysseus proceeds in a very orderly fashion, almost without malice.

Eurymachus tries to attack Odysseus, but he is stopped by an arrow through the breast. He falls across the table, knocking it, the food, and the wine to the floor. Amphinomus tries his luck only to be struck from behind by Telemachus' spear. Telemachus goes to his father's side and tells him that he will get armor and more spears. Odysseus keeps the suitors at bay until his son returns. He, Telemachus, Eumaeus, and Philoetius are now armed. Before his arrows run out Odysseus slays many of the suitors. Agelaus, who has so far escaped death, seeks a way of summoning reinforcements. Melanthius, the goatherd, explains that the exits are barred, but that he might be able to sneak out of the hall and go to the storeroom where the armor and spears are kept-with arms they might have a better chance in the battle.

When Odysseus sees the suitors putting on the armor that Melanthius has brought, he grows fearful. Eumaeus spies

Melanthius returning to the storeroom for more weapons and follows him. There, he and Philoetius overpower Melanthius and leave him hanging from the ceiling by a rope around his middle. The disloyal goatherd hangs there until the end of the fighting, at which time he is killed.

Athena, in the guise of Mentor, now enters the hall. Odysseus asks her to fight on his side (he is fairly certain that it is Athena he sees before him). Agelaus seeks to frighten her away by threatening to kill her after Odysseus has been slain. Athena, of course, is not frightened by Agelaus, but is angered by Agelaus' threat. She spurs Odysseus on to finish the slaughter, then leaves without taking an active role in the fighting.

Agelaus, in a last-ditch attempt, rallies five other suitors to throw their spears at Odysseus in the hope of wounding him with at least one. Odysseus, however, avoids all six spears. He and his three companions now return the throw, killing four of the six attacking suitors. Again the suitors attack, again they are driven back. Telemachus and Eumaeus receive scratches in this attack, Telemachus on his wrist, Eumaeus on his shoulder, but both are able to keep fighting.

Leodes rushes forward unarmed and clasps Odysseus' knees in the traditional manner of the suppliant. He asks to be spared on the grounds that, as the suitors' priest, he was not responsible for their actions and that he never molested any of the women in the house. Odysseus refuses to accept this excuse and cuts him down. Now Phemius, the minstrel, pleads for his life. He tells Odysseus that he never sang for them voluntarily, but was always dragged to the house. Telemachus speaks up in Phemius' behalf and also asks that Medon, the herald, be spared. Odysseus agrees not to slay these two men, and now realizes that all the suitors have been killed.

Comment

Two persons only are spared in Odysseus' blood bath. The first, Medon, is a herald, who holds an office usually held sacrosanct and inviolate. Heralds operated under truce flags and carried messages between feuding and warring parties. If Medon were alive today, he would be a Swiss ambassador. The second person spared is Phemius, a minstrel, and so a man in the same profession as Homer. For Homer it would obviously be bad form to have a minstrel die at the hands of his own hero. In addition Homer apparently considered Phemius and all minstrels above local politics and family quarrels. The killing of the suitors here, like that of Odysseus' crew by the Laestrygonians in Bk. 10, is compared to shooting fish in a barrel. Odysseus, on the other hand, is now, as before, described as a raging lion.

Odysseus summons Eurycleia and asks her who of the maidservants has remained faithful. There are twelve, says Eurycleia, who have adopted shameful ways. Bring them here, says Odysseus. When they come, he has them remove the bodies and clean the hall, which is splattered with blood and gore. After they have finished, Telemachus takes them outside and hangs them by the neck so that they may die as painfully as possible. Melanthius is now killed. The slaughter is over. Odysseus is now ready to face his wife.

BOOK 23

Eurycleia happily climbs the stairs to tell her mistress that her husband is home. Wake up, she cries from the foot of the bed, your husband is back and he has killed all the suitors. Penelope accuses her of having lost her wits. I'm not joking, insists the nurse, he really is here. Penelope demands to know how he could have killed all of the suitors.

Comment

Penelope hesitates to accept the truth, much as she would like to. By asking what Odysseus did, if he is home, she keeps his presence hypothetical.

Eurycleia says that she does not know how he killed them, and again asks her to come and see for herself. Even the mention of the scar on his leg does not convince Penelope that Odysseus is his own avenger. She suspects that some clever god has disguised himself as the beggar and has slain the suitors (she has already accepted the notion that the suitors are dead). When Penelope finally leaves her room, her thoughts are in a turmoil-should she embrace her husband or keep aloof? She decides to keep aloof, and when she comes face to face with him, she can only stare first at his face, then at his rags.

Telemachus cannot understand what is holding his mother back from sitting near, or even talking to, her husband. She replies that she is still not sure that he is Odysseus and that she will test him when they are alone. More important to Odysseus than convincing Penelope of his identity at that moment is to make certain that the families of the slain suitors do not find out what he has done before he can prepare for them. He suggests that they all put on new clothes and orders Phemius to play his lyre, so that, if anyone passes by outside, there will be no indication that anything is amiss. This plan works so well that the people who pass by think that Penelope has chosen a husband.

Odysseus, meanwhile, has finished bathing, and once more sits opposite Penelope. She now tests him to see whether or not he is truly her husband. She asks Eurycleia to move her bed. Odysseus shouts in anger at this request. He himself had built the bed around a living olive tree and if the bed can be moved it means that Penelope has cut away the tree.

> **Comment**

This is the third time that an olive tree has been mentioned in association with sleep.

Odysseus' anger gladdens Penelope's heart, for only he, she, and a maid knew of the bed's construction. Now certain of her husband's identity, she pleads with him not to be angry with her for having tested him. The two embrace, but the thought of having to travel further still troubles Odysseus. He confides in Penelope that Teiresias (Bk. 11) had told him that after arriving in Ithaca, he must travel inland with an oar on his shoulder until someone should mistake his oar for a fan for winnowing wheat. He is then to plant the oar in the earth, sacrifice a bull, a ram, and a boar to Poseidon, and return home, where, after many years, he will meet a peaceful death. But the thought of this journey cannot lessen the happiness Penelope feels as she and Odysseus lie in bed together for the first time in nineteen years.

> **Comment**

Ever since the third century B.C., there have been people who think that the *Odyssey* ends at this point, with hero and heroine finally united. They believe that everything which follows the reunion was composed by someone else and added to the poem. But the style of the **epic**, as seen in the *Iliad*, as well as in the *Odyssey*, is to follow the **climax** with the tying up of loose ends. The families of the slain suitors are still to be reckoned with, and Odysseus must be reunited with his father. There is no reason to believe that the post-climactic details are written by anyone's hand but Homer's.

Odysseus now tells Penelope of all his adventures, starting with the Cicones (Bk. 9) and ending with his stay among the Phaeacians (Bk. 13). Sleep overtakes them both at the end of the long story. The next morning Odysseus tells Penelope that he is off to see his father and that she must stay in her room until he returns. He wakes up Telemachus, Eumaeus, and Philoetius, who accompany him to his father's house.

BOOK 24

This book opens in the underworld, where Hermes, the traditional guide of the dead, is leading the souls of the dead suitors to their destination. On the way they pass Agamemnon and Achilles, two heroes of the *Iliad* (see Bk. 11), who are discussing the old days. Achilles recalls Agamemnon's sad death at the hands of his wife; Agamemnon, in turn, recalls Achilles' glorious death in battle and his magnificently royal funeral.

Comment

This bit of small talk makes us realize what a romance the *Odyssey* is. Achilles and Agamemnon lived as heroes, but they are dead now (we have already heard from Achilles in Bk. 11 how dreary death is). Odysseus, too, was a hero in the Trojan War; but he, unlike Achilles, survived the war. Odysseus, too, had a wife to come home to; but his wife, unlike Agamemnon's, remained faithful. In addition, he had many exciting adventures. In other words, Odysseus has had the best of all possible experiences as a soldier, adventurer, and lover.

Achilles and Agamemnon stop their talk when they see the host of newcomers to the land of the dead. Agamemnon recognizes Amphimedon (one of the six men Agelaus marshaled against Odysseus, in Bk. 22) and asks him what **catastrophe** brought so many men to their deaths. Amphimedon replies in great detail, telling him of their attempt to woo Penelope, how she fooled them by weaving and then unweaving the shroud, and how Odysseus, disguised as a beggar, slew them all with the aid of his son. Agamemnon applauds Odysseus for having such a faithful wife-one who surpasses his own wife, Clytemnestra, in every possible way.

Meanwhile, Odysseus and his companions have reached Laertes' farm. Odysseus has grown so cautious that even though there is no longer any danger, he still hesitates to tell his father the truth. Pretending, therefore, to be a stranger to Ithaca, he asks Laertes where he can find Odysseus whom he befriended many years ago. The mention of his son brings tears to Laertes' eyes. He asks Odysseus who he is and receives yet another lying tale from his son's inventive mind. But now Odysseus can no longer bear to see his father in such grief. He reveals his true identity and tells him that he has slain the suitors. Laertes is naturally suspicious of this man who claims to be his son. He asks for proof. Odysseus shows him the scar on his leg and, in addition, tells him the exact number of pear, apple, and fig trees Laertes planted when Odysseus was a boy. Laertes, now convinced that this is truly Odysseus, warns him of the relatives and friends of the suitors who will seek revenge. Odysseus tells him not to worry about it and suggests that they go to the house to eat. At the house, Odysseus is greeted warmly by Laertes' servants.

But back at the palace the news has finally leaked out about the death of the suitors. An assembly is hastily called, at which

Eupeithes denounces Odysseus for having caused the death of his crew and of the suitors. He suggests that they punish Odysseus before he escapes (as if Odysseus would be afraid of these men!).

Medon and Phemius, the only two men Odysseus spared, now approach. Medon tells the assembly that Odysseus was helped by a god who pretended to be Mentor. Halitherses, one of the old men present, who can see the future, vouches for Medon. The gods, he says, are on Odysseus' side. He suggests that they abandon their plan to take vengeance on Odysseus. But most of them are after Odysseus' life, and they rise to arms.

Athena, who has observed this assembly, asks Zeus for advice. Zeus says that Athena is, to a large extent, responsible for this situation and that she should do as she sees fit. He does, however, have a plan: let the suitors' families swear an oath of allegiance to Odysseus so that he may rule in peace ever afterwards. But while the two immortals are discussing the matter, the angered brothers and fathers of the suitors reach Laertes' farm. Athena has time to rush to Odysseus' side, again in the form of Mentor. Odysseus turns to his son and asks him to fight his hardest and so bring honor to their house - a challenge Telemachus readily accepts. Laertes is overjoyed to see his son and grandson preparing for battle together.

So uplifted is he that all traces of his former despondency disappear. He is able, with the first spear of the battle, to slay Eupeithes. Odysseus and Telemachus join in the fight and are about to kill all the enemy when Athena calls a halt to the fighting. The Ithacans drop their weapons, but Odysseus is in such a rage that he prepares to leap on them as an eagle would leap on his prey. He is stopped only by a lightning bolt hurled down by Zeus. Athena once more orders him to stop. Odysseus obeys. Peace is now established in Ithaca.

Comment

This last picture of Odysseus, almost crazed with his lust for vengeance, is truly exciting. Compare it with the first time we see him, on Calypso's island, sitting in tears by the seashore, eager to be home once more. He is home now, back in the real world, and his every wish has been granted.

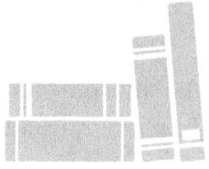

THE ODYSSEY

STRUCTURAL ANALYSIS

Scholars who analyze the structure of the *Odyssey* see that it is divided (like Gaul) into three parts: Bks. 1-4, the so-called Telemachia, or adventures of Telemachus, son of Odysseus; Bks. 5-12, the sea adventures and travels of Odysseus; and the nostos or return of Odysseus to Ithaca. Such clear breaks or distinct sections have led some scholars to believe that the *Odyssey* is a compilation of three different myths, sagas, or legends in one long **epic** by someone named Homer.

ODYSSEUS AS JAMES BOND

Solid critical scholarship has lately focused on the Homeric character portrayal of individual actors, particularly the **protagonist** Odysseus. Though many of the characters from the *Iliad*, particularly Achilles, Hector, and Ajax are more heroic, Odysseus offers the critic a most interesting superego or persona. He is noble (when it is useful), crafty, unprincipled, vicious, and unfaithful (while his wife is faithful). While the closed society of heroic Greek culture speaks only to itself at most levels, the wondrous and exciting world of Odysseus goes across time and strikes the modern reader as a modern story. Achilles is god-like; Odysseus is like James Bond, and we prefer the latter.

FRYE AND CAMPBELL ON HOMER

Odysseus is on a journey, dramatically from Troy to Ithaca, actually from birth to death, metaphysically from death to life. In his *Anatomy of Criticism*, Northrup Frye observes that "of all fictions, the marvellous journey is the one formula that is never exhausted." Once Homer had established such a "marvellous journey" in the *Odyssey* Bks. 5-12, no **genre** of Western literature ever moved far away from it for very long. It is too much a part of reality and real life, of imagination and day-dreaming. Odysseus goes off to war, undergoes terrible ordeals and tests, and returns to Ithaca a more potent force than when he left. He leaves as the ruler of an island kingdom; he returns the most famous adventurer of all times. The journey was his own personal rite de passage. Joseph Campbell has made this type of "marvellous journey" the core of his famous work, *The Hero with a Thousand Faces*:

The standard path of the mythological adventure of the hero is a magnification of the formula represented in the rites of passage: separation-initiation-return: which might be named the nuclear unit of the monomyth. A hero ventures forth from the world of common day into a region of supernatural wonder: fabulous forces are there encountered and a decisive victory is won: the hero comes back from this mysterious adventure with the power to bestow boons on his fellow man.

Though the *Odyssey* has a clearly marked tripartite structure (Bks. 1-4; 5-12; 13-24), there is an underlying organizing principle which (observed even by a biologist like Aristotle) gives true cohesion to the long **epic** and direction and purpose to its myriad of adventure stories. Homer chose as the efficient motif of the *Odyssey* the wrath of Poseidon. Because of an offense against the deity, Odysseus is made to wander over the Mediterranean Sea for ten years after the end of the Trojan War (1184-1174 B.C. according to ancient reckoning). This organizing motif gives the *Odyssey* a sense of purposeful direction, and after Odysseus is freed from Poseidon's curse, a successful **denouement** to the adventure story is at hand.

NEW LINES OF INQUIRY

Those critics not interested in the historical-archaeological aspects, the "Homeric Question", oral composition, or classical polemics, but interested in more literary discussions, have begun to tackle the *Odyssey* along the lines of its constituent parts. In the first place we realize that the *Odyssey* is connected to the saga at Troy - and so to the *Iliad*. The whole background of the *Odyssey*, the reason for Odysseus' voyage lies in the dim past of Mycenaean legend and the saga of the warriors and sea-raiders who sailed off to Troy at the command of Agamemnon to ravage and plunder the coastal cities in Asia Minor. The inquiring critics are fast at work in analyzing the original contributions of Homer and his unique handling of traditional materials. A second group of critics is busily engaged in dealing with the sea adventures of Odysseus between his wars at Troy and his return to Ithaca. In view of the later successes of sea stories including their famous captains like Nemo and Ahab, it is appropriate to turn careful criticism on the role of the sea in ancient Greek society. Since no point in Greece is more than 35 or so miles from the sea, the Greek view of the sea, its possibilities for life and for death, must have exerted a terrible influence on the emerging literary minds-one of which was Homer's. A third group of critics is looking into the matter of Odysseus' homecoming, i.e., the last twelve books. This whole **epic** and the homecoming section especially, is very much like a novel (or a romance) in verse. Our hero leaves his small island (picture it as a small town in the South), journeys to Troy (picture it as a large urban city in the North) and after becoming very famous, cynical (perhaps jaded is the term), and middle-aged, he returns home-only to find that you cannot ever go home again. After reclaiming his kingdom, killing the suitors of his wife, and reestablishing his absolute rule, Odysseus learns (it is fated) that he must embark on another long and dangerous voyage. His journeys are innumerable and will last forever. Odysseus is a permanent exile, allowed to return home for brief visits only. Perhaps Odysseus reflects in some way a wandering minstrel named Homer who travels all over Greece pursuing elusive goals. The hero of Campbell's "monomyth" returns home and performs some valuable service. Here Campbell stops his study; but Odysseus cannot stop or rest. He is driven out by forces inside and outside, a wandering Jew before the Jews were wandering. Perhaps the most interesting group of critics working on the *Odyssey* is the fourth, which takes as its starting point the difference in outlook and spirit between the *Iliad* and the *Odyssey*. In general terms, the *Iliad* is a work in honor of the hero, the man with absolute arete, the man who lives to do honor to himself. Achilles and Ajax stand out because they can perform better on the field of combat than any other men. Arete and victory in battle are the songs of the fireside minstrels in the *Iliad*. Heroism and the hero in the *Odyssey* are different. Odysseus is not the young, dashing Achilles of the *Iliad*. He is middle-aged, perhaps paunchy, tired after twenty years of war and travel, an exile. The fame of Odysseus does not rest on arete but rather on craftiness, stealth, his way with words, his cunning, and his lack of scruples with friends, enemies or wife. The *Odyssey* is the **epic** of adventure and travel, not the epic of great battles and the destruction of great cities. Odysseus travels to enchanted islands and makes love to enchanted princesses. He probes the depths of Hades, survives Scylla and Charybdis, tricks the Cyclops Polyphemus, and is shipwrecked more often than St. Paul. The *Iliad* is the **epic** of Greek men and warriors, the *Odyssey* of Everyman. The character Odysseus operates on many levels, as opposed to a cardboard hero. He is father, husband, lover, warrior (underhanded), tricky, and, at the end of the *Odyssey*, a murderer. He is surely more than Greek, and his appeal extends beyond heroes.

MODERN VIEW OF HOMER'S GODS

E. R. Dodds, in Chapter I of *The Greeks and the Irrational*, gives a modern interpretation of the role of the gods in Homer. To the earlier critics, the gods were comic figures, merely clowns who interfered whenever they could in the affairs of mortals. These critics found in the poems evidence of Greek disbelief in human free will. They pointed out that scarcely a fight or council occurs without some god interfering and influencing events.

By carefully examining all the examples of divine intervention, Professor Dodds concludes that the gods were used by Homer to explain extraordinary events and actions. Thus, when a warrior shoots an arrow farther than usual, the warrior will say that Ares, god of war, pulled back the bowstring for him. This can be the only explanation for his having shot so well. The gods were used to explain bad actions as well as good ones; for example, when Penelope refuses to choose a suitor, Antinous says that the gods have put the idea of refusal into her head (Bk. 2). The characters in Homer's poems believed that through the gods they could explain all acts that weren't rational; that is, that were not the normal actions of a normal mortal. Anything out of the ordinary must, they reasoned, be the result of a god's machination.

Homer, the poet behind the characters, had the power to make the gods appear. Thus, if a character interpreted the flight of an eagle to be a propitious sign from Zeus, Homer could, and usually did, show us Zeus sending forth the eagle. It is but a short step beyond this to have gods visible to us, the audience, and not visible to the characters they are affecting. An example of this is Mentor's advice to Telemachus (Bk. 2). His advice is so apt that Homer feels that it must be ascribed to a god (Athena, in this case), even though Telemachus seems willing enough to accept the advice as the words of a mortal.

Odysseus, the craftiest of mortals, constantly has Athena, the goddess of craft, by his side aiding him whenever she can. But this does not detract from Odysseus' stature. In fact, it enhances his stature, for what Athena's presence indicates is that Odysseus' powers are so much beyond ordinary mortals that they can only be explained in terms of divine help. This is great praise indeed. Athena is the natural choice for Odysseus' divine champion since she is the ageless ideal of reason-Odysseus' great characteristic.

But the Greek gods are not merely literary devices to explain unusual attributes and occurrences. They have personalities as well developed as any mortal's. They are subject to the same emotions that rule all men. They even quarrel and fight among themselves.

AUERBACH ON HOMER'S DIGRESSIONS

There is another aspect to Homer's technique that should be examined. This is his habit of interrupting the flow of the narrative with digressions that, seeming to have little to do with the point in question, tend to retard the flow of action. This can be disconcerting to a modern reader, who expects events to proceed uninterrupted. The modern reader does not expect to find, for example, a battle scene in which, in addition to the fighting itself, a great deal of attention is given to the genealogies of minor characters. Authors after Homer were careful to "set the scene" by describing the characters beforehand so that in a tense scene they were not obliged to introduce new characters for the first time. But these later authors were writing their works. They had time, before their work was read, to rearrange the scenes so that everything seemed "natural" and so that the narrative and story flowed without interruption.

Homer, on the other hand, was not working with the written word, but with the oral **epic**. He couldn't erase or rearrange what he had spoken. This does not mean that the poem proceeded without plan or that there was no unity to the whole work; what it does imply is that as Homer recited, certain words would trigger associations which Homer would then present in a digression, always making sure to return to the point from which he had departed.

Not only men but also inanimate objects would receive this treatment. A bow brought into battle, for example, might be given as full a history as any warrior's, being traced back in some instances to the god Hephaestus. Just as Homer increases the stature of a warrior who plays a minor role by endowing him with noble ancestors, so he increases the stature of a bow (or any other weapon) which is about to slay a mighty warrior. The fact that the digression concerning the soldier or the object lessened the tension did not bother Homer, for tension and suspense played little part in his story. This technique of stress through digression never became a mechanical device. If it had, every important object would have come complete with a genealogy.

Erich Auerbach, in *Mimesis* (see Bibliography), discusses Homer's use of digression and compares it with the terse style of the Old Testament. He maintains that Homer describes objects as fully as he does because of a need to externalize everything; that is, to present everything in full perspective. But this cannot be the full answer, for obviously Homer cannot externalize all objects that he mentions. Auerbach never asks the question why some objects are elaborated upon while other objects are not.

Auerbach chooses as his example the **episode** in Bk. 19 where Eurycleia first notices Odysseus' scar and realizes that the beggar she is washing is Odysseus. But, between her first notice of the scar and her recognition of her long-lost master, there are seventy-four lines of explanation concerning the origin of the scar. Only after the digression do we learn that Odysseus was successful in stopping Eurycleia from telling Penelope of her husband's return (here, by the way, is an example of a digression that heightens the suspense, although this is not Homer's main purpose). Auerbach says that Homer will not let the scar appear out of an unilluminated past but insists on spot-lighting it with a story out of Odysseus' boyhood. He pursues the content of the digression no further.

DIMOCK ON ODYSSEUS' SCAR

The story of the scar is examined more fully by George E. Dimock, Jr., in his article "The Name of Odysseus," first published in *The Hudson Review*, IX (Spring, 1956) and recently reprinted in two paperback collections of essays (see Steiner and Fagles in the Bibliography). The story told in the digression is the following:

Odysseus was given his name by his grandfather Autolycus, who had a reputation for being a thief and a liar. The name "Odysseus" was connected, in Autolycus' mind, if not in linguistic fact, with the word odyne, "pain." "Since I have caused pain to many men," said Autolycus, "let us name him Odysseus, 'Pain'" (or "Trouble" as Dimock translates it). Once when Odysseus visited Autolycus, he and his uncle went on a boar hunt. The boar was a cunning beast and charged Odysseus, gashing the young man's thigh before he could be stopped by Odysseus' spear. The gash left a distinctive scar which Eurycleia recognized.

The **episode** of the boar hunt is a vindication of the name Autolycus chose for his grandson. Here is Odysseus living up to his name in full, both giving pain and receiving pain at the same time. Professor Dimock sees in this act the essence of Odysseus' identity. Throughout the poem, Odysseus is hurting people, directly and indirectly, consciously and unconsciously. He is constantly looking for conflict and struggle. He is most unhappy in situations which would delight other men. Calypso's isle, for example, is a paradise which few men would willingly leave. Yet Odysseus shuns Calypso's offer of immortality on the heavenly isle and risks an inglorious death-drowning in solitude-in order to escape life without end-which, to Odysseus, is life without meaning.

Odysseus is the unwitting cause of grief to his parents, wife, and son. His father, preoccupied with his longing for his son, withdraws to his farm; his mother dies in grief (a grief which reflects back on Odysseus when he meets her in the underworld); his wife is subjected to the wooing of the unruly suitors because of his prolonged absence; and his son is subject to their insults and plots. Odysseus brings most pain, of course, to his crew and to the suitors, and herein lies another key to an understanding of the *Odyssey*. For Odysseus, while he causes trouble, is no mere trouble-maker. Only through conflict (which invariably causes pain) can he be truly involved with life, life in the sense of social life, not life in nature, for man has been battling nature for all of history. There is no honor in being overwhelmed by the sea: conflict means involvement with men not nature.

Odysseus pits himself against all comers in tests of wit and strength. He is an example of the new individual who was developing in Ionia (the Dorians, to the west, retained their old communal spirit). In the *Odyssey*, we see Odysseus, an individual, in conflict with the old communal order. The suitors and their families want Penelope to remarry so that community life might resume. In this, they are within their rights. But Penelope will have none of it: she waits for Odysseus despite the needs of the community. Her individuality is as strong as her husband's. She brings to mind Odysseus' speech to Nausikaa, when he first meets the young Phaeacian: "There is nothing finer or more fitting than when man and wife, in constant agreement, rule their house, causing pain to their enemies." The contrast between Odysseus and the crew and the suitors is made even clearer in the similes. Homer constantly compares Odysseus to lions and eagles, beasts that travel alone with their families. The suitors and the crew, on the other hand, are compared to fish, which travel in schools. Another link between the crew and the suitors, which at the same time presents another contrast between Odysseus and the community, is that both the suitors and the crew, against the wishes of Penelope and Odysseus, slay cattle.

PORTER ON THE ODYSSEY AS POEM OF REBIRTH

The *Odyssey*, then, is Odysseus' search to find his place in the world. Throughout the poem, his search is described in terms of rebirth (this is discussed by Howard Porter in his introduction to the Bantam edition of the *Odyssey*; see Bibliography). When we first see Odysseus, he is at a low point in his travels, waiting dejectedly on Ogygia, Calypso's island. Even the two names are ominous. "Ogygia" means "primeval," "primitive"; "Calypso" means "concealer." Odysseus is being concealed from the real world on an island so far removed from humanity that even Hermes complains of its loneliness. It is a struggle for Odysseus even to reach the fairyland worlds of the Phaeacians, Cyclopes, Lotus-eaters, etc., no less the real world of Ithaca, where he will be "reborn."

Odysseus' journey does not take him directly from Ogygia to Ithaca in either fact or symbol. He must first undergo several periods of danger and near-death. His journey to the underworld is the climactic symbol of his closeness to death. Professor Porter points out that the olive tree is mentioned in three of these "death" **episodes** and that these three episodes occur at transition points in the poem. The first of these **episodes** occurs at the end of Bk. 5, when Odysseus, naked, seeks protection under two olive trees. In the succeeding books, Odysseus, who started out naked, becomes richly clothed with gifts. But he must be reborn once more in Ithaca. The Phaeacian sailors who bring him to Ithaca drop him off in a protected harbor. They place Odysseus, who has fallen into a death-like sleep, at the base of an olive tree. Odysseus must elevate himself once more, this time from beggar to king. The third olive tree is the one that forms a post of his bed. It is his knowledge of this tree that finally establishes his true identity to Penelope, so that once again he is "reborn," this time with Penelope at his side.

HOMER'S INFLUENCE

If you can comprehend the influence of Shakespeare, you are well on the way toward grasping the influence of Homer, who had a 2400 year head start on the Bard. By the fifth century B.C. in Greece (Homer, ca. 800 B.C.), the *Iliad* and the *Odyssey* together made up the Greeks' Old and New Testaments. Homer became the absolute dominant literary, religious, and social force. In the fourth and third centuries B.C. his influence waned as rationalism and kepticism overwhelmed the minds of the Greeks, and the Alexandrians with their short, allusive, and esoteric poems held the day. Apollonius of Rhodes (221-181 B.C.) in his **epic** the *Argonautica* changed much of Homer's classical restraint into the romantic and sentimental. School boys and literate men continued to worship Homer, but the Alexandrians and Apollonius had blunted some of Homer's force. Homer continued to be the mine from which the tragedians took their stories and plots, and the mythographers their myths. Socrates quotes Homer in that fatal court trial for his life, and Alexander, thinking himself another Achilles, carried a copy of the *Iliad* with him on his journeys. Homer's greatest influence on the Greeks, however, is seen in the unifying force he unleashed which bound the Greeks together, gave them a common book to read, made them feel that being Greek was more important than being Mycenaean or Athenian or Theban, provided a common language, and gave them a common background and historical past.

Homer moved into the Roman world as a mighty influence, and one of the earliest pieces of Latin literature is Livius Andronicus' translation into verse of Homer's *Odyssey*. Latin literature had its beginnings in the reflection of Greek, and at that beginning stood Homer. Vergil was Homer's greatest admirer and patterned his *Aeneid* so carefully after the *Iliad* and *Odyssey* that, had it been written today, Vergil could be sued for breaking the copyright laws. In defense of Vergil, however, we should add that in the ancient world imitation (later centuries it became **parody**) was the highest form of flattery, and creative imitation the highest form of art. The next **epic** writer after Vergil, Lucan (39-65), in his *Pharsalia* altered drastically the Homeric mode of **epic**: he removed the myth from its central role, removed the traditional gods to a large extent (**deus ex machina**, etc.), and made historical narratives, in this case the civil war between Caesar and Pompey, the center and substance of the **epic**. In his *Thebaid*, Statius (45-96) returned to the Homeric mode. The "pupils" of Homer, Vergil and Statius, remained very popular throughout the Middle Ages and the Renaissance.

In the ancient world Homer had a great influence not only on the literary set but also on the simple-minded and lower classes. One example suffices: John Scott in his book *Homer and his Influence* (1925) has isolated twelve Homeric passages in one short piece of the New Testament! Clearly it was expected that even Christians were supposed to have read Homer.

Because Latin was the language of the western Middle Ages and a knowledge of Greek was confined to Constantinople, parts of the Byzantine Empire, and Greek settlements in southern Italy, Homer in Greek was unknown, while Vergil was known by all. During the Renaissance, however, this changed when the knowledge of Greek returned to the West. Even Dante was forced to learn of Homer from Latin sources. We can date the arrival of Homer in Greek in the West with some certainty to 1354, for at that time Petrarch acquired a Greek manuscript of the **epic** from Constantinople. From this Greek manuscript Leontius Pilatus made a Latin prose translation from which Petrarch and Boccaccio learned of Homer first hand. The first printed edition of Homer appeared in 1488 in Florence, and thereafter editions appeared in rapid succession in Venice, Rome, Strassburg, Basel, and after a century's delay in London in 1591.

HOMER'S INFLUENCE IN ENGLAND

Chaucer knew Homer only through secondary sources but in his *House of Fame* pays him homage:

Ful wonder hye on a pileer Of yren, he, the greete Omere.

Spenser borrowed from Homer for his *The Faerie Queene*, and from *Troilus and Cressida* we can see that Shakespeare was at least acquainted with Chapman's famous translation of Homer. In *Comus* and *Paradise Lost* especially we detect Milton's debt to Homer, who, like Dante's Vergil, almost became Milton's Christian pagan. Pope translated the *Iliad* and Dryden produced a critical essay on Homer in addition to translating *Iliad* Bk. 1.

Beginning with the eighteenth century and extending to the first half of the twentieth, Greek was a necessary language for any English gentleman-especially the Cambridge-Oxford gentleman. Classical education held the day in that enlightened age. Byron asked that *Don Juan* be compared with Homer's works:

My poem is **epic**, and is meant to be After the style of Virgil and Homer, So that my name of **epic** is no misnomer.

And Keats wrote a **sonnet** "To Homer" as well as one on Homer and Chapman, "On First Looking into Chapman's Homer", which celebrated Chapman's famous translation. Tennyson, too, loved Homer and we can see clearly the influences of Homer's *Odyssey* in his "The Lotus-Eaters" and "Ulysses". It is interesting to add that the famous English prime minister, Gladstone, wrote several critical essays on Homer. In those happier days even politicians had been educated before leaving school.

HOMER IN THE TWENTIETH CENTURY

The twentieth century has become so familiar with Homer, and his *Odyssey* is so influential, that the word "Odyssey" has become synonymous with adventurous travel. The Greek National Airlines advertises a "Greek Odyssey" for the daring traveler, and Earl Selby has entitled his book about trips through Black ghettos, *Odyssey: Journey Through Black America*. In a marvelous adventure story (which formerly was called science fiction), *2001: A Space Odyssey*, Arthur Clarke translates Odysseus' fantastic land and sea journey into a space trip by a group of astronauts. Stanley Kubrick then gave Clarke's story a new medium and produced one of the most thrilling and visually stimulating motion-pictures ever made. Kubrick neatly portrays adventurers going through uncharted regions, recalling for us that when Odysseus sailed over the Mediterranean Sea he was as far from "civilization" as the astronauts in *2001: A Space Odyssey*. The wonders in space were no more startling than the wonders Odysseus beheld on uncharted islands. The adventures of the astronauts and of Odysseus both have magical, marvelous, and unbelievable episodes-especially to the uninitiated reader who must enliven his life by reading and cannot personally or physically partake of the unknown.

HOMER IN THE ARTS

For those readers interested in the effect of Homer's *Odyssey* on the arts (except for literature, we can direct them to several interesting works: W. B. Stanford, "Representations of Ulysses in the Visual Arts," in his *The Ulysses* **Theme**; Walter Agard, *Classical Myths in Sculpture*, gives a survey of the classical influence on contemporary plastic arts: Monteverdi used the story of Odysseus' journey as the structure for his opera *Il Ritorno d'Ulisse in Patria*. Those students and readers of Homer's *Odyssey* who

THE ODYSSEY

wish to see firsthand (almost) the "wine dark" Mediterranean and islands Odysseus visited are fortunate to have at present several extraordinary books available. We recommend especially Erick Lessing's fantastically beautiful *The Adventures of Ulysses: Homer's **Epic** in Pictures* and Maurice Obregon's *Ulysses Airborne*. Those interested in a word-picture journey to retrace Odysseus' steps will be richly rewarded to make their excursion with Ernle Bradford, *Ulysses Found*, in his small sail boat.

HOMER AND EASY RIDER

The all-pervasive influence of the *Odyssey* on literature and the arts has been illustrated with special insight by Charles Saylor in his essay, "*Easy Rider*: A Contemporary *Odyssey*:"

The overall journey of *Easy Rider* can be described as an involuted *Odyssey* because it ends in an underworld rather than a homecoming. Its overall tone is pessimistic, its heroes finally revealed as anti-heroes, the thrust of their adventure misdirected and finally frustrated because of wrongs both in society and in the nature of heroes.

Saylor goes on to compare the types of journeys in both stories, the drug culture and the land of the Lotus-Eaters, the rational Odysseus and his irrational men vis-a-vis the rational lawyer George and Captain America and the irrational Billy. The importance of pastoral **themes** both in the *Odyssey* and in *Easy Rider* is dealt with at some length and this points up values of goals in both works. In *Easy Rider* the wanderers admire the bucolic life of ranchers but cannot summon up the determination to settle in the unspoiled part of the country. Later they take the irrational approach and resume a purposeless wandering. Odysseus' wandering is apparently purposeless but, while in *Easy Rider* the cosmos is out of control, in Homer's world there is true order-temporarily out of commission. Odysseus is seeking a home of familiarity, of pastoral quiet and simplicity, to end his wanderings. The travelers in *Easy Rider* are driven about by outside circumstances, which in the *Odyssey* had been personified as Poseidon, and in search of something to which they can attach themselves. But finding this, they reject it and move on to something else. In a real sense they are a type of "wandering Jew," travelers on a perennial odyssey, a "Flying Dutchman" without a ship.

ODYSSEUS THEME IN JOYCE AND KAZANTZAKIS

Of all the contemporary works based on Homer's *Odyssey* the most famous, influential, and widely read are James Joyce's *Ulysses* (1922) and Nikos Kazantzakis' *Odyssey* (1938). Kazantzakis borrowed little or nothing from Joyce. The works of both are highly original, but in going back to classical **themes** are conservative in their own ways. We believe that the two radically different approaches to the same classical stimulus of Homer can be accounted for by recalling that Joyce was Irish and Kazantzakis Cretan. The main difference between Joyce's Leopold Bloom (*Ulysses*) and Kazantzakis' Odysseus is their modes of travel and adventure. Bloom's adventures and deeds of valor take place in his mind and thoughts, and his heroism is one of ambition and potentiality, not reality. Kazantzakis' Odysseus lies closer to Homer's character since both are men of action, resource, and physical abilities.

KAZANTZAKIS' SEQUEL

Kazantzakis' *Odyssey* is full of travel and adventure. It begins roughly where Homer's work leaves off. Odysseus returns home but, realizing that his son Telemachus cannot live under his long shadow, soon departs from Ithaca and travels to Sparta where he encourages a peasant revolt and steals Menelaus' wife (Menelaus has grown fat and lazy), and sails to Crete and Egypt, where he again encourages local revolts and traces the Nile to its source. After founding a city and watching its subsequent destruction, Odysseus becomes a mystical figure with special connections to the deities, and at the same time he has also become more lonely, more separated and cut off from his fellow man-in the Greek sense, more heroic. In a very mystical scene Odysseus dies and goes off to become part of the gnostic or Stoic fire of life. Odysseus is a man in search of freedom, personal freedom, and knowledge, self-knowledge. The search for this freedom leads Odysseus into a kind of ascetic life, where freedom means a separation from the social life so dear to all Greeks. This separation leads Odysseus away from human intercourse to the sea where he dies. Though many **episodes** in Kazantzakis' work are products of his own fertile imagination and not borrowed from Homer, the inspiration for the story and the travels as well as the character of Odysseus are Homeric. Odysseus the exile, the wily hero from the island of Ithaca, is he the marvelous adventurer reflecting Kazantzakis' (also from an island) alter ego? Are all Greek writers exiles? Is Odysseus really Everyman in search of a place to die, a reflection of Everyman in the rites de passage from birth to death?

JOYCE'S PARALLELS

James Joyce's *Ulysses* is so well known to every literate man of the Western world, and itself so influential, that it perhaps might seem peculiar to look at the literary influences behind it. These influences are surely legion. Only one is of concern to us here, the influence of Homer. In addition to a map of Dublin, the reader of Joyce's *Ulysses* should have a copy of Homer's *Odyssey* close at hand. The exact parallels between Homer and Joyce and the borrowings of the latter from the former have been documented and perhaps over-documented.

Joyce apparently had been interested in Homer's *Odyssey* since a boy, for, when asked to write an essay on his favorite hero, he chose Odysseus. Later in this same Odysseus he saw the universalized measure of man for all occasions, a harried modern man. But Leopold Bloom, Joyce's interpretation or rather re-working of a Greek figure, is a particularly un-heroic type, except perhaps for the heroic actions which take place in his mind. Many of the ancient writers including Homer felt that their age was one worth praising. Joyce's opposition to this is a clear break with his Greek source. It is extremely difficult to make any kind of hero out of Leopold Bloom, an advertising canvasser, or, for that matter, out of Stephan Daedalus. "Always evasive when confronted by action, Joyce shuns heroics. The relation of the *Odyssey* to *Ulysses* is that of parallels that never meet. The Homeric overtones do contribute their note of universality, their range of tradition, to what might well be a trivial and colorless tale. But in so doing, they convert a realistic novel into a mock-epic" (Harry Levin, *James Joyce*).

To give a small illustration of how carefully Joyce patterned the structure of *Ulysses* on Homer's *Odyssey,* we can list the following parallels (a very small fraction of the total number of parallels): the *Odyssey* was written in 24 books while *Ulysses* covers a period of only 24 hours. In general the following characters are drawn from Homer: Bloom is a modern Odysseus; Molly Bloom is as faithful as a modern Penelope can be; Bella Cohen is the sorceress Circe and provides a high point in *Ulysses*, as she had done in the *Odyssey*; Odysseus' long affair with Calypso is reduced to a shadowy affair with

Martha Clifford (after all, unheroic man should have affairs with unheroic women only!); Sinn Feiner, the attacker of Bloom, is Polyphemus; and Kierman's pub is the cyclops' cave; and lastly, Gerty MacDowell is a type of Nausikaa. Detailed literary studies of *Ulysses* are readily available and have the space to consider the thousands of relationships between the two works.

THE ODYSSEY

ESSAY QUESTIONS AND ANSWERS

Question: How have scholars set the date of composition for the *Odyssey*?

Answer: The *Odyssey* was originally an oral **epic** (a poem to be recited from memory). Since scholars have established that only in illiterate societies can poets recite from memory poems of great length, it is reasoned that the *Odyssey* was written down shortly after writing was introduced (while poets still lived who were accustomed to reciting and composing from memory).

Through the study of inscriptions (gravestones, official decrees, writing on implements, etc.) it has been determined that 800 B.C. is the approximated date for the introduction of writing to Greece. The date for the *Odyssey*'s composition is therefore also set at 800 B.C.

Question: How can we estimate the dates of the events of the *Odyssey*?

Answer. Since Odysseus' wanderings date from the end of the Trojan War, it is with the dates of that War we must concern ourselves. Up until the nineteenth century (and the "discovery" of archaeology), the accepted date of the War, handed down from antiquity, was 1184 B.C. With the unearthing, however, of the many levels of Troy, it became the scholars' task to determine which level was the Troy of the Trojan War. One level, VIIa, showed evidence of a siege, was destroyed by fire, had two embattled skeletons lying out in the open, and was inhabited during the time pre-archaeology historians estimated the Trojan War occurred. From surviving relics, archaeologists were able to assign a date to level VIIa - that date is 1250 B.C., the very date given by the Greek historian, Herodotus. If the Trojan War was fought in 1250 B.C., Odysseus' wanderings took place between 1250 and 1230 B.C.

Question: Why does Athena prefer Odysseus to all other mortals?

Answer: Homeric gods operate on several levels. They are "immortal mortals" subject to the same passions and emotions which rule mortal men. But they are also these emotions and passions personified. Ares, for example, is not only the god of war, he is war itself. When a soldier says Ares has helped him he means a) Ares was present in physical form to give aid; and b) he (the soldier) was imbued with the spirit of war.

Athena is the goddess of skill and craft. Enamored of her own talents, she naturally admires them in mortals - and Odysseus is the most skillful and crafty of all mortals. (Think of her delight in Odysseus' lying tale [Bk. 13] when he attempts to hide his identity from her, mistaking her for a shepherd.) Athena is so delighted with Odysseus' clever deception, that she praises him in words that set him above all mortals. She leads the gods in cleverness; he leads the mortals.

As the personification of skill and craft, Athena is present in Odysseus far more than in any other mortal. To praise him for his guile and cleverness is to say that Athena is in him, and since he encompasses more of Athena than does any other human, she is a large part of him, so she naturally favors him.

Question: The time scheme of the *Odyssey* is complicated. Can you justify Homer's free use of time?

Answer. The entire *Odyssey* takes place in less than six weeks. Between the time that Telemachus leaves Ithaca and Odysseus defeats the angry "insurgents" is only a matter of 40-41 days. But within this 40-day framework, Homer includes the history of the past 19 years. We eventually learn about the ten-year Trojan War, the fate of the Greek heroes, and Odysseus' adventures during the nine years following the war.

Homer jumps in at the tail end of Odysseus' wanderings, 40 days before the hero reaches home. Odysseus is alone and weeping on Calypso's deserted isle. When he leaves the isle he will return to the real world, leaving behind him enchanted isles, one-eyed giants, sorceresses and cannibals. Homer chooses this moment for his point of departure because it is the most significant moment in Odysseus' wanderings-he has been tested, he has ventured, suffered, triumphed, and now he will return, reborn, to the home of his fathers.

The fantasy adventures over the past nine years are symbolically important, but the man Odysseus, the hero in the real world, is even more important-we meet him first and through flashback we hear of Odysseus in fairy land.

Question: How does Homer keep Odysseus at the center of focus throughout the epic?

Answer: Even when we are watching other characters, our attention is continually drawn back to Odysseus through

Homer's intended use of comparison and contrast. If we look at a few examples (they are legion), we will see how Homer sometimes overtly and sometimes by implication relates subsidiary characters to Odysseus.

Telemachus

When we first meet Telemachus, he is at the mercy of the suitors because of his father's long absence. When, with Athena's urging, he convenes an assembly, he sits in Odysseus' seat and tries to emulate his father. We are invited, directly, to compare the ineffectual young man with his forceful father.

Agamemnon

We hear frequently throughout the **epic** of Agamemnon's sorry fate (and we twice meet him in Hades). Agamemnon, like Odysseus, was a Greek warrior who distinguished himself of Troy. Like Odysseus, Agamemnon had a family to return to after the War. But when Agamemnon reached home he was slain by a faithless wife and adulterous cousin. We immediately think of the faithful Penelope and adoring Telemachus when we hear Agamemnon's story. How blessed our hero is, despite all is suffering during his travels.

The Lotus-Eaters

Although the Lotus-eaters are a people without strife, their lack of conflict, their withdrawal from the world has left them almost inhuman. Odysseus, a perfect example of the striving, questing, adventurous mortal, enriched and challenged by interaction and contract, makes these tranquil people seem moribund. The comparison is unavoidable.

The Crew

Except for one or two spokesmen, the members of the crew are scarcely distinguishable one from the other. As a unit, they are frequently in disagreement with Odysseus. The men of the crew function as a gregarious, dependent community. Odysseus stands alone. He is the tough-minded, distinct individual concerned with himself and his own welfare. The contrast between the independent Odysseus and his highly dependent crew is continually brought to our attention.

Penelope

We never see the expectant wife without thinking of the lost husband. Like Odysseus, Penelope is concerned with her own welfare even at the cost of the community's well-being. Penelope almost matches her husband in wit and guile and when she deceives (as with the shroud) or tests her fellows (as she tests Odysseus with the bed-post), we immediately think of the craftiest mortal-her teacher and husband Odysseus.

ANNOTATED BIBLIOGRAPHY FOR THE ODYSSEY

Translations And Editions

Butcher, J. H., and Lang, A., *Odyssey*. New York: Random House (1879).

Butler, Samuel. *Homer: The Odyssey*. Translation revised by Malcolm M. Willcock. Supplementary materials prepared by Walter James Miller. New York: Washington Square Press (1969). The supplementary materials include sections on Homer's techniques and style, characterization, maps of Homer's world and of Odysseus' and Telemachus' journeys, a pronouncing guide and index, etc.

Cook, Albert, *Homer: The Odyssey*. New York: Norton, 1967.

Fitzgerald, Robert, *The Odyssey*. New York: Doubleday, 1961.

Lattimore, Richard, *The Odyssey*. New York: Harper & Row, 1967.

Palmer, George, *The Odyssey*. New York: Bantam, 1963.

Palmer's translation is preceded by a brilliant introduction by Howard Porter, who discusses the **epic** as a poem of rebirth.

Rieu, E.V., *The Odyssey*. Harmondsworth: Penguin, 1962.

Shaw, T.E. (T.E. Lawrence, "Lawrence of Arabia"), *The Odyssey of Homer*. Oxford: Oxford University Press, 1932.

Primary Works

Auerbach, Erich, *Mimesis*. Princeton: Princeton University Press, 1953.

Bassett, Samuel, *The Poetry of Homer*. Berkeley: University of California Press, 1938.

Beye, Charles, *The Iliad, the Odyssey, and the **Epic** Tradition*. New York: Doubleday, 1966. The best short introduction to Greek epic.

Bowra, C. M., *Heroic Poetry*. London: Macmillan, 1952.

Carpenter, Rhys, *Folk Tale, Fiction and Saga in the Homeric Epics*. Berkeley: University of California Press, 1946.

Clarke, H. W., *The Art of the Odyssey*. Englewood Cliffs: Prentice-Hall, 1967.

Combellack, F. M., "Contemporary Unitarians and Homeric Originality," *American Journal of Philology* 71 (1950) 337-364. Powerful arguments for the theory that Homer composed both the *Iliad* and the *Odyssey*.

Finley, M. I., *The World of Odysseus*. London: Chatto, 1956.

Hainsworth, J. B., *The Flexibility of the Homeric Formula*. Oxford: Oxford University Press, 1968.

Hansen, William, *The Conference Sequence: Patterned Narration and Narrative Inconsistency in the Odyssey*. Berkeley: University of California Press, 1972.

Hoekstra, A., *Homeric Modifications of Formulaic Prototypes*. Amsterdam: Noord-Hollandsche, 1965.

Hoekstra, A., *The Sub-Epic Stage of the Formulaic Tradition*. Amsterdam. Noord-Hollandsche, 1969.

Jaeger, Werner, *Paideia: The Ideals of Greek Culture*. New York: Oxford University Press. 1939.

Kirk, G.S., *The Songs of Homer*. Cambridge: Cambridge University Press, 1962.

Knight, W. F. J., *Many-Minded Homer: An Introduction*. London: Allen, 1968

Lord, Albert, "Homer, Parry, Huso," *American Journal of Archaeology* 52 (1948) 34-44. A study of oral composition.

Lord, Albert, *The Singer of Tales*. Cambridge, Mass., Harvard University Press, 1960.

Lord, Albert, "Composition of **Theme** in Homer and South Slavic Epos," *Transactions and Proceedings of the American Philological Association* 82 (1951) 71-80.

Lorimer, H. L., *Homer and the Monuments*. London: Macmillan, 1950.

Myers, John, *Homer and his Critics*. London: Routledge, 1958.

Nilsson, Martin, *Homer and Mycenae*. London: Methuen 1933.

Page, D. L., *The Homeric Odyssey*. Oxford: Oxford University Press, 1955.

Parry, Milman, *The Making of Homeric Verse: The Collected Papers of Milman Parry*, ed. Adam Parry. Oxford: Oxford University Press, 1971. Parry's important works are included in this volume along with an English translation of his French dissertation. Parry was surely the most original scholar to work on Homer in this century. To him we owe our concept of Greek **epic** as oral composition.

Parry, Milman, *L'Epithete traditionnelle dans Homere*. Paris: Les Belles Letters, 1928.

Parry, Milman, "Studies in the **Epic** Technique of Oral Verse-Making. I: Homer and Homeric Style," *Harvard Studies in Classical Philology* 41 (1930) 73-147; and "II: The Homeric Language as the Language of an Oral Poetry," 43 (1932) 1-50.

Parry, Milman and Albert Lord, *Serbocroatian Heroic Songs*. Cambridge: Harvard University Press, 1954. About 20 volumes are in preparation. Translation of the Parry collection of Serbocroatian **epics** recorded in 1934-35. The actual voice recordings reside at Harvard on 2500 aluminum discs.

Pocock, L. G., The Sicilian Origin of the Odyssey. A Study of the Topographical Evidence. Wellington: Wellington University Press, 1957.

Pocock, L. G., *Reality and Allegory in the Odyssey*. Amsterdam: Hakkert, 1959.

Pocock, L. G., *Odyssean Essays*. Oxford: Blackwell, 1965.

Schipp, G. P., *Studies in the Language of Homer*. Cambridge: Cambridge University Press, 1972.

Scott, J. A., *The Unity of Homer*. Berkeley: University of California Press, 1921.

Scott, J. A., *Homer and his Influence*. Boston: Marshall Jones, 1925.

Seymour, T. D., *Life in the Homeric Age*. New York: Macmillan, 1907.

Snell, Bruno, *The Discovery of the Mind*. Cambridge, Mass.: Harvard University Press, 1953.

Thornton, A., *People and **Themes** in Homer's Odyssey*. London: Methuen, 1970.

Wace, Alan and F. Stubbings, *A Companion to Homer*. London: Macmillan, 1962.

Webster, T. B. L., *From Mycenae to Homer*. London: Methuen, 1958.

Whitman, C. H., *Homer and the Heroic Tradition*. Cambridge, Mass.: Harvard University Press, 1958.

Woodhouse, W. J., *The Composition of Homer's* Odyssey. Oxford: Oxford University Press, 1930.

Secondary Works

Bartok, Bela and, Albert Lord, *Serbo-Croatian Folk Songs*. New York: Columbia University Press, 1951. An account of the **epics** as folk songs in the Serbo-Croatian areas.

Bradford, Ernle, *Ulysses Found*. London: Hodder, 1963. The author takes a small sailing boat and retraces the adventures of Odysseus in his wanderings.

Butler, Samuel, *The Authoress of the Odyssey*. London: J. Capi, 1925.

Clarke, Arthur, *2001: A Space Odyssey*. New York: New American Library, 1968.

Dimock, George J., See Steiner and Fagles, *Homer, A Collection of Critical Essays*.

Donington, Robert, "Return of Ulysses," *Times Literary Supplement* (4 August 1972) 913. The story of the revival and return to the repertoire of Monteverdi's (1567-1643) opera Il Ritorno d'Ulisse in Patria.

Foerster, D. M., Homer in English Criticism: The Historical Approach in the Eighteenth Century. New Haven: Yale University Press, 1947.

Gordon, C. H., *Homer and the Bible. The Origin and Character of East Mediterranean Literature. Ventnor, N.J.: Ventnor, 1967.*

Graves, Robert, *Homer's Daughter.* New York: Doubleday, 1955.

Grosvenor, Melville, "The Isles of Greece: Aegean Birthplace of Western Culture," *National Geographic* 142 (1972) 147-193. Fantastic pictures and excellent maps of the world of Odysseus.

Kazantzakis, Nikos, *The Odyssey: A Modern Sequel*, trans. K. Friar. New York: Simon and Schuster, 1958.

Lessing, Erick, *The Adventures of Ulysses: Homer's **Epic** in Pictures.* New York: Dodd, Mead, 1970. 71 colored plates; 9 are two-page spreads. A fantastic color view of the Greece Odysseus might have seen.

Obregon, Maurice, *Ulysses Airborne.* New York: Harper and Row, 1971.

Porter, Katherine Anne, *A Defense of Circe.* New York: Harcourt, Brace, 1954.

Saylor, Charles, "*Easy Rider:* A Contemporary *Odyssey*," Classical Bulletin 48(1972) 81-85.

Selby, Earl and Miriam, *Odyssey: Journey Through Black America.* New York. Putnam, 1971.

Stanford, W.B., *The Ulysses **Theme**.* Oxford: Blackwell, 1963.

Steiner, George and Robert Fagles (eds.). *Homer, a Collection of Critical Essays.* Englewood Cliffs: Prentice-Hall, 1963.

Taylor, C.H., editor, *Essays on the Odyssey.* Bloomington: University of Indiana Press, 1963.

www.ingramcontent.com/pod-product-compliance
Lightning Source LLC
LaVergne TN
LVHW012057070526
838200LV00070BA/2785